ROAD TO THE VINEYARD

Cruising Through
New Jersey
Wine Country

CHARLIE TOMS

Road to the Vineyard: Cruising Through New Jersey Wine Country

Writing and photography by Charlie Toms

Artwork by Kelly Walton and James Watkins

ISBN 978-0-9908267-0-5

Printed in USA by 48HrBooks (www.48HrBooks.com)

Table of Contents

In memory of my Aunt Janet who loved to visit places in New Jersey, and inspired me to do great things.

Foreword

Like many road trips, my journey with New Jersey wine was unplanned and took many unsuspecting turns. For most of my life, I have had an interest in places in New Jersey, and as a child my mother took me on plenty of road trips to local attractions.

I drank my first New Jersey wine at age 21. I was on vacation in Wildwood, and I was looking for something to do on a rainy day. I read about Cape May Winery, but I couldn't get any information on it. This is when the Internet was new, and most businesses did not have websites. The local tourist bureau and chamber of commerce had heard about the winery, but couldn't tell me where it was located.

With a good map and information from a winery guide, I found Cape May Winery, but it was not open to the public. The owners told me that production was limited and they sold their wine to a single restaurant. I had no interest in the restaurant, but I decided to eat there and order a bottle of Cape May Chardonnay. I don't remember the food that night, but the wine was worth writing home about.

Until this point, I was a beer man. I had just graduated from Drew University, and beer had always been the drink of choice at college. In my mind, wine was a beverage of snobs that came from exotic locales, cost too much, and didn't taste good. This bottle of wine was different. It was made by local farmers, cost less than $10, and actually went far better with dinner than beer.

For a number of years, I attended festivals sponsored by the Garden State Wine Growers Association (GSWGA), and drove to various wineries in the state. Sometimes I would go with family members, sometimes with friends. The three things that I always noticed were the state's broad selection of wine varieties, how much fun everyone had on wine trips, and the spectacular beauty of the New Jersey countryside.

About two years ago, I became curious about how many wineries there were in the state. When I first started drinking New Jersey wine, there were seventeen wineries. However, in the last decade, the state's wine industry has experienced exponential growth. Nowhere could I get a straight answer to my question. The GSWGA site listed all their members, but I knew of a handful of independent producers. Every wine book and online winery directory gave a different answer.

I decided to do my own investigation, and in the process I found that a lot of published information about wineries was missing or erroneous. Even a basic question about when a winery went into business was challenging. Some wineries listed the year they started selling to the public. Some listed when they made their first wine. Some listed when the grapes were first planted. One listed their founding date as when the owner first dreamed about being a vintner!

I did a lot of research, and I wrote Wikipedia articles about each of the state's 48 wineries. I wanted a way for the public to get unbiased information about an industry where facts are hard to come by. Besides shine a light on individual wineries, the articles allowed me to get a broad view of the state's wine industry. I had read that around 30 types of grapes were used in New Jersey, but when I compiled the production data for each vineyard, I found more than 90 different grapes being used for wine production.

The Wikipedia articles had a litany of information about founding dates, types of winery licenses, varieties of grapes under cultivation, the number of cases produced each year, etc. However, I wanted to write more. A bunch of encyclopedia articles may be informative, but wine is meant to be enjoyed, not just studied.

I took a paid correspondent position with the American Winery Guide. Jim Finley founded the American Winery Guide in 2007 because he had taken a wine trip to California, and like me found that there was a severe lack of information about American wineries. My AWG articles were just as factual as my Wikipedia articles, but allowed me to review individual wines and give a vivid description of each place. Each winery I have visited has a unique history, ambience, and selection of wines.

This book is themed on the PBS travel series *Spain – On the Road Again*. In that show, chef Mario Batali, actress Gwyneth Paltrow, food writer Mark Bittman, and actress Claudia Bassols travel around Spain in a Mercedes convertible. They ate the best food, drank the best wines, and lived life to the fullest. I encourage people to do the same here. Travel around New Jersey, visit its beaches, mountains, and other attractions, and enjoy the state's diverse array of culinary and cultural events.

The first chapter of the book is an overview of the history of wine in the Garden State and the current status of the New Jersey wine industry. Since this is primarily a guide for tasting New Jersey wine, I keep the history section short. For those interested in a detailed historical account of the state's viticulture, I suggest reading Sal Westrich's *New Jersey Wine: A Remarkable History.* The remainder of my book tells a story about each of the 48 wineries currently in business.

I sort the state's wineries geographically into four regions with a total of eight possible road trips. Some of these wine trails are intuitive, such as the six wineries in Cape May County that form an almost straight line north to south. Other trips are more subjective, and some readers may want to mix and match. For some people, visiting six or seven wineries in a day may be a bit overwhelming. These wine trails are merely suggestions.

Each road trip lists some potential places to eat and lodge. As a general rule, I avoid chain restaurants and hotels, and try to provide the reader with establishments that offer a unique experience. Since many readers may be travelling with children or family members that are not as interested in wine, I mention some other attractions to visit. Many of the places in this book are hidden gems, and are not crowded or overpriced.

In the end, let your road trip be spontaneous. If you see something unusual on the way, stop and visit it. If you're having a great time at a winery, stay there and drink more. The first time I visited wineries near Atlantic City, I stopped to see a shrine of Saint Padre Pio. I always stop at interesting restaurants or roadside food stands during my journeys, and I list some of these places in the book. Start up your cars, and now let's begin our adventure.

History and Overview

Nobody knows exactly when the first wine was produced in the Garden State, but in 1642 Johan Björnsson Printz, the Governor of New Sweden, told his people to make wine from wild grapes. Much of what was New Sweden is today the extremely fertile farmland of southwestern New Jersey.

In 1767, the Royal Society of Arts offered a prize of 200 pounds sterling (around $600,000 in modern money) to Edward Antill for wines that he produced on his Piscataway estate. That being said, early New Jersey was better known for hard cider and applejack, and there was little commercial wine production in the state until the Civil War.

Wine would boom in New Jersey in the late nineteenth century. In 1849, Concord grapes were developed in Concord, Massachusetts from native *labrusca* vines. They can be grown in areas with cold winters, and though looked down upon by wine aficionados both then and now, heavily-sweetened Concord wine became popular among the general public.

Hiram Dewey, a wine merchant from New York City, planted a vineyard in Egg Harbor City in 1857, triggering a wave of wine production in southern New Jersey. To escape the phylloxera (an aphid-like insect) epidemic destroying grape vines in Europe, Louis Renault immigrated from the Champagne region of France to New Jersey, and in 1870 Renault Winery open to the public.

Renault Winery soon became the largest producer of champagne in the United States, producing a half of million cases per year at its peak. Besides commercial wineries, there were thousands of small farms in New Jersey where families grew grapes and made wine for their own personal consumption. Waves of Italian and German immigrants settled in New Jersey and brought their winemaking traditions with them.

A fungicide made of lime and copper sulfate was developed that largely eliminated the bane of black rot that had long plagued grape growers. A 1909 report by the State Board of Agriculture indicated that more than three million pounds of wine grapes were being harvested annually in the Garden State. The same report indicated that New Jersey winegrowers were reaping a very healthy 18% profit margin on their crop.

While natural problems with viticulture were being conquered, winemakers of the twentieth century would face a bigger problem – the government. Temperance movements had long been active in the United States, but they were generally more concerned with hard liquor than wine. However, after the turn of the century there was a move to ban all alcohol production. Winemakers, brewers, and distillers were often vilified as foreign profiteers.

Prohibition went into effect in 1919 with the passage of the Volstead Act. Although alcohol consumption was still legal and though some towns in the state openly flouted the law by issuing liquor licenses, the law was a disaster for the state's winemakers. A few like Renault survived by getting permits to make wines for medical or religious use, but when Prohibition was repealed, only three Garden State wineries (Dewey, Renault, and Kluxen) remained.

The decades following Prohibition were almost as bad for the state's wine production. The state established the Alcoholic Beverage Control Law which imposed a litany of rules on liquor producers and distributors, including a limit of one winery for every million residents. That would restrict the number of wineries in the state to a handful.

After World War II, improved transportation created competition from high-end European vintages and the burgeoning California wine market. Only three new wineries were founded in New Jersey between 1930 and 1970 – Balic, Tomasello, and the now-defunct Jacob Lee Winery. Dewey Winery would close in 1952, Kluxen Winery went out of business in 1973, and by the mid-1970s Renault was on the edge of bankruptcy.

A small number of dedicated unlikely individuals would emerge to save the state's wine production from extinction. Michael Fisher was a prominent scientist at Merck who planted grapes in Hunterdon County after reading about viticulture in *Scientific American* magazine. Fisher banded with several other winemakers from northwestern New Jersey to form the Hunterdon Winegrowers Association.

This organization, which later became the Garden State Wine Growers Association, persuaded the legislature to pass the Farm Winery Act of 1981. This law created a less expensive license for small-scale wine producers that use only New Jersey grapes, and eliminated population-based restrictions on the number of wineries. A year later, Amwell Valley Vineyard (now known as Old York Cellars) would receive the first winery license issued under the new law.

Frank Salek was a civil engineering professor at the New Jersey Institute of Technology who believed that the climate of Southern New Jersey was similar to that of Bordeaux, and that it was possible to make European-style wines from grapes grown in the Garden State. The handful of wineries that operated in the state in the 1970s mostly produced sparkling wines or dessert wines from French hybrid or native *labrusca* grapes.

Salek carefully selected an area that had the correct climate and soil, and exclusively planted *vinifera* grapes. Many of the established winemakers in the state thought that Salek was on the road to financial ruin. He personally grafted European vines onto phylloxera-resistant roots, and founded Sylvin Farms Winery. Salek would become one of the most famous winegrowers in the state, and other vintners would use his techniques to grow *vinifera* grapes.

The 1980s would be an era of growth and improvement for New Jersey viticulture. Besides Amwell Valley and Sylvin Farms, within a year or two after the passage of the Farm Winery Act, a number of wineries including Alba Vineyard, Four Sisters Winery, and Unionville Vineyards would be founded. Many of the new wineries were in northwestern New Jersey, and were started by people who were interested in scientific winemaking. The goal was quality not quantity.

Around the year 2000 when I started drinking New Jersey wine, there were 17 wineries in the state, with most of them being in Atlantic, Hunterdon, and Warren counties. The Garden State Wine Growers Association held a handful of festivals of year. However, many people I met didn't even know that the state had wineries. A number of the vineyards had very limited tasting hours, and were not open in the winter. At the time, New Jersey's winegrowers often seemed more like a hobby association than an industry.

The twenty-first century has been a renaissance for the New Jersey wine world. Since 2001, more than thirty new wineries have opened their door. Some like Bellview, Heritage, and Cedarvale, existed for generations as a fruit farms, but faced stiff competitions from giant agribusinesses from California and South America. Others like Auburn Road Vineyards were founded by people who lacked farming and winemaking experience but had plenty of ambition.

Today there are 48 New Jersey wineries operating in 13 counties. I am glad to report that no Garden State winery has gone out of business in the last ten years. These wineries produce nearly two million gallons of wine per year from an astounding 95 different grapes and 29 other fruit. There are at least 25 wine festivals and wine trail weekends each year, and after a few years of battling, the state's vintners regained the right to ship wine to customers.

Besides volume, New Jersey is becoming a hotspot for high-quality wine. Unionville's Chardonnays have taken top prizes in national and international competitions. Recently, famed wine reviewer Hugh Johnson named Alba Vineyard as one of the country's "leading estates." In 2012, eight wineries participated in the Judgment of Princeton, a blind tasting where $20 wines from New Jersey outperformed $600 French vintages.

I am optimistic about the future of New Jersey wine. I suspect that the number of wineries in the state will continue to grow, albeit a slower rate than in the last decade. While there are perennial grumbles about the quality of wine coming from newer winemakers, my experience is that many vineyards start with wines that are easier to make and have mass appeal, and then explore more complex vintages until they find their niche. Today is definitely the best time to be either a New Jersey winegrower or a New Jersey wine drinker.

Introduction to the Skylands

The Skylands is the mountainous northwestern region of the state, consisting of Sussex, Warren, and Hunterdon, and parts of Morris and Passaic counties. With its rocky soil and cold snowy winters, this area may not be where you expect to find grapes growing. However, Kluxen Winery operated in the town of Madison from 1865 to 1973, and today there are twelve wineries operating in this region. Some of the most famous wineries in the state, such as Alba Vineyard, Four Sisters Winery, and Unionville Vineyards are in the Skylands.

There are two American Viticultural Areas for the Skylands – Warren Hills and Central Delaware Valley. However, only five of the twelve wineries in this section are located in a viticultural area, which reflects that the borders were drawn back in the 1980s before the massive expansion of the New Jersey wine industry. Because of the weather and soil, native *labrusca* grapes like Concord and French-American hybrid grapes like Vidal Blanc predominate here. Most of these wineries are part of Vintage North Jersey, a subsidiary of the Garden State Wine Growers Association.

The first six wineries are in Sussex County and the northern half of Warren County. This wine trail includes treks through the steep hills and dense woods of the Kittatinny Mountains, passing through oft-forgotten small towns like Belvidere and Hamburg. Much like the area, the wineries of the northern Skylands are often simple and unpretentious. As a result, the tasting rooms are typically less crowded, and unrushed service and friendly conversation are the norm.

The remaining six wineries are in southern Warren County and Hunterdon County. This area includes spectacular vistas along the Delaware River, trendy historic villages like Frenchtown, and miles of pastoral countryside. The southern Skylands have been a core wine producing area for more than three decades. This region's wines have won top awards in national and international competitions, and I would argue that this road trip offers the best white wines in the state.

Road Trip #1

Wineries:

1. Westfall Winery
2. Ventimiglia Vineyard
3. Cava Winery & Vineyard
4. Brook Hollow Winery
5. Four Sisters Winery

Restaurants/Eateries:

Granny's Pancake House and Grill – Three generations of women run this cozy eatery which offers homestyle cooking and very friendly service. Besides a wide selection of pancakes and other breakfast fare, Granny's makes really good burgers and sandwiches.
Address: 181 Hamburg Turnpike (Route 23), Hamburg, NJ
Phone: (973) 827-2390

Hot Dog Johnny's – Since 1944, hot dogs have been sold from this iconic roadside stand which backs onto the scenic Pequest River. Hot Dog Johnny's sign advertising French fries, birch beer, and buttermilk is classic Americana from a bygone era, and their prices seem equally frozen in time.
Address: 333 Route 46, Belvidere, NJ
Phone: (908) 453-2882

Red Wolfe Inn – While the exterior looks like an abandoned garage, this place has some of the best steaks in the state, less common selections like trout and escargot, and an extensive array of imported and microbrew beers. Afterwards, check out the real wolves enclosed in the back.
Address: 130 Phillipsburg Belvidere Road (Route 519), Belvidere, NJ
Phone: (908) 475-4772

Lodging:

Apple Valley Inn – Nestled in the heart of the Pochuck Valley less than a mile from the Appalachian Trail, this 1831 country inn is bound to charm. The property comes complete with a store that sells twenty varieties of candied apples, and a creek with a wooden footbridge.
Address: 967 McAfee-Glenwood Road (Route 517), Glenwood, NJ
Phone: (973) 764-3735

Camp Taylor – This is one of the best places for camping in New Jersey. The site offers 400 acres of pristine forest, a beautiful lake for swimming, and well-maintained cabins and RVs. Camp Taylor is also the home to the wolves, foxes, and bobcats of the Lakota Wolf Preserve.
Address: 85 Mount Pleasant Road, Columbia, NJ
Phone: (908) 496-4333

Attractions:

High Point State Park – At 1803 feet above sea level, this is the highest spot in the state. High Point Monument adds another 220 feet, and provides a spectacular view of three states – New Jersey, New York, and Pennsylvania. In the summer, swimmers can enjoy the cool, spring-fed waters of Lake Marcia.
Address: 1480 Route 23, Sussex, NJ
Phone: (973) 875-4800

Land of Make Believe – This place was founded by a music teacher who wanted an amusement park where parents could interact with their children. The Land of Make Believe favors low-tech, non-frightening rides, and is much more family friendly than many corporate-run parks.
Address: 354 Great Meadows Road, Hope, NJ
Phone: (908) 459-9000

Westfall Winery

   Westfall Farm in Montague has been in business for over 200 years. Founded in 1774 by Simon Westfall, it was formerly a stop on the Underground Railroad and a dairy farm. The Mortimer family bought the farm in 1940, and they still own it. In 2000, Loren & Georgene Mortimer planted grape vines, and three years later, the winery opened to the public. The Mortimers also own a winery in Hilton Head, South Carolina.

   Westfall is in a very rural area at the top of New Jersey near High Point State Park. Besides wine, the farm offers horse boarding, specializing in the Morgan breed, and the Mortimers also raise Black Angus cattle. The owners and staff are very friendly, and when I visited earlier this year, they were offering barrel tastings for many of their wines. Though not always available, I recommend their Chocolate Orange Port. Made from Petite Sirah and aged for three years, this unique port is 18% alcohol, and has the aroma of citrus and the smoothness of chocolate.

Address: 141 Clove Road, Montague, NJ

Phone: (973) 293-3428

Website: www.westfallwinery.com

E-mail: westfallwinery@gmail.com

Appellation: N/A

Associated Winery: Island Winery (South Carolina)

First vines planted: 2000

Opened to the public: 2003

Key people: Loren & Georgene Mortimer, Charles Mortimer (owners)

Acres cultivated: 6

Cases/year: 9,000

Grapes: Cabernet Franc, Cabernet Sauvignon, Cayuga White, Chardonnay, Concord, Durif (Petite Sirah), Grenache, Merlot, Mourvèdre, Muscat of Alexandria, Niagara, Pinot Gris, Pinot Noir, Riesling, Sangiovese, Syrah, Tempranillo, and Zinfandel

Other fruit: apples, blackberries, blueberries, cranberries, and peaches

Other attractions: pet-friendly, picnicking, horse boarding.

Days: tastings Friday to Sunday in summer, Saturday and Sunday in spring and fall, closed in winter except for events.

Ventimiglia Vineyard

Gene Ventimiglia has been producing wine for his family's personal consumption for over three decades. In 2002, he planted a vineyard in a heavily forested part of Wantage, and six years later, Ventimiglia Vineyard opened. The winery focuses on quality over quantity, advocating artisanal winemaking techniques, including producing only small batches of wine, and using minimal chemical or mechanical intervention.

The tasting room is in a cute ranch-style house with a patio behind it. While visiting, I met Gene's son Anthony who was preparing new vintages. It is the only winery in New Jersey that produces wine from Carignan, Frontenac Gris, La Crescent, and Sumoll – Frontenac Gris and La Crescent are white hybrid grapes developed in Minnesota, whereas the other two varietals are red *vinifera* grapes indigenous to Spain. I liked their Cabernet Franc, which is aged in French and Hungarian oak, and would go perfectly with lamb chops.

Address: 101 Layton Road, Wantage, NJ

Phone: (973) 875-4333

Website: ventivines.com

E-mail: gene@ventivines.com

Appellation: N/A

First vines planted: 2002

Opened to the public: 2008

Key people: Gene & Anne Ventimiglia, Anthony & Myla Ventimiglia (owners)

Acres cultivated: 5

Cases/year: 1,000

Grapes: Cabernet Franc, Carignan, Cayuga White, Chambourcin, Chardonnay, Chenin Blanc, Concord, Durif (Petite Sirah), Frontenac Gris, Grenache, La Crescent, Merlot, Pinot Noir, Sangiovese, Seyval Blanc, Sumoll, Syrah, Traminette, Vidal Blanc, and Zinfandel

Other fruit: N/A

Other attractions: pet-friendly, picnicking

Days: tastings on weekends

Cava Winery & Vineyard

Cava Winery is not just a place to taste wine, but a place to really enjoy wine. Anthony Riccio planted grapes in Hardyston in 2005, and the winery opened three years later. Winemaker Jeff Blake oversees production. The winery is named for the Italian word *cava* which means "cave," reflecting the mining heritage of Sussex County. In July 2012, Cava was profiled on the TV show *Road Trip with G. Garvin*. The winery has a separate brand for their fruit wines, named "Ceci Bella" after the owner's dog.

I had tasted Cava's wine before, but visiting their facility was a unique experience. Guests are seated at bistro-style tables and can order flights of wine and light food to accompany it. It is the only winery in New Jersey that uses Ciliegiolo, Grechetto, and Sagrantino, which are *vinifera* grapes from the Umbria region of Italy, and the only place in the state to produce wine from açaí berries, pears, and watermelons. My favorite was Açaí Raspberry Cabernet Sauvignon, which has the body of a Cabernet, the sweetness of raspberries, and tropical flavors of açaí.

Address: 3619 Route 94, Hamburg, New Jersey

Phone: (973) 823-9463

Website: www.cavawinery.com

E-mail: info@cavawinery.com

Appellation: N/A

Other labels: Ceci Bella

First vines planted: 2005

Opened to the public: 2008

Key people: Anthony Riccio (owner); Jeff Blake (winemaker)

Acres cultivated: 5

Cases/year: 3000

Grapes: Cabernet Franc, Cabernet Sauvignon, Ciliegiolo, Chardonnay, Durif (Petite Sirah), Grechetto, Merlot, Muscat Blanc, Pinot Gris, Pinot Noir, Riesling, Sagrantino, Sangiovese, Sauvignon Blanc, Trebbiano, and Zinfandel

Other fruit: açaí berries, apples, blackberries, blueberries, kiwifruit, peaches, pears, pomegranates, raspberries, strawberries, and watermelons

Other attractions: bistro

Days: tastings and tours on weekends

Brook Hollow Winery

Although Paul Ritter has made wine for his family's consumption for many years, he never expected to be a professional vintner. In 2002, he planted two thousand grape vines in his yard. Five years later, he leased land from a fruit farmer near the village of Columbia in Warren County, and started Brook Hollow Winery. In 2013, Brook Hollow moved across town to a new location. Yards Creek runs through the original property, and formed the hollow for which the winery is named.

The tasting room is a chalet-like structure with an outdoor patio overlooking the vineyard. Because of the region's mountainous climate, Ritter primary grows cold-hearty grapes. They are the only winery in the Garden State to use Geneva Red, which is a red hybrid grape developed in New York in 1947. Brook Hollow makes two wines for which a quarter of the sales go to benefit the nearby Lakota Wolf Preserve. I recommend their Cabernet Franc, which is dry but oaky and strong-bodied, and can be paired with a grilled steak.

Address: 594 Route 94, Columbia, NJ

Phone: (908) 496-8200

Website: www.brookhollowwinery.com

E-mail: winemaker@brookhollowwinery.com

Appellation: Warren Hills

First vines planted: 2002

Opened to the public: 2007

Moved to new location: 2013

Key people: Paul Ritter (owner)

Acres cultivated: 8

Cases/year: 1050

Grapes: Cabernet Sauvignon, Cayuga White, Chambourcin, Chancellor, Chardonnay, Concord, Frontenac, Geneva Red, Merlot, Riesling, Vidal Blanc, and Zinfandel

Other fruit: cranberries

Other attractions: weddings

Days: tastings Tuesday to Sunday

Four Sisters Winery

Some years ago, I participated in a murder mystery dinner at Four Sister Winery where the wine was not the murder weapon. In fact, the wine was very good, a tribute to Robert "Matty" and Laurie Matarazzo who first planted grapes on their 250-acre fruit farm in White Township in 1981. Three years later, they opened the winery which is named after their four daughters. Besides murder mystery dinners, Four Sisters has Aunt Sadie's Bakery and Café which sells pies and sandwiches in the autumn.

Four Sisters is the only winery in New Jersey that produces wine from Delaware, Léon Millot, and Marquette, which are red hybrid grapes with a tolerance of cold weather. The winery also grows a number of other fruits that they use to make wine. My favorite wine was their Cedar Hill Rosé, a sweet *labrusca* blend that would go perfectly at a picnic. When I visited, Four Sisters was offering tastings of some of their original vintages, and I had the pleasure of trying their 1981 rosé, which was just as sweet but had an even smoother finish.

Address: 783 North Bridgeville Road (Route 519), Belvidere, NJ

Phone: (908) 475-3671

Website: foursisterswinery.com

E-mail: mattyfla@gmail.com

Appellation: Warren Hills

First vines planted: 1981

Opened to the public: 1984

Key people: Robert "Matty" & Laurie Matarazzo (owners)

Acre cultivated: 8

Cases/year: 5000

Grapes: Baco Noir, Catawba, Cayuga White, Chambourcin, Concord, Delaware, Frontenac, Léon Millot, Marechal Foch, Marquette, Niagara, Seyval Blanc, Traminette, and Vidal Blanc

Other fruit: apples, cherries, blueberries, pumpkins, raspberries and strawberries

Other attractions: bakery, corn mazes, fruit picking, pet-friendly, picnicking, weddings

Days: daily tastings except on Wednesdays

Road Trip #2

Wineries:

1. Alba Vineyard
2. Villa Milagro Vineyards
3. Mount Salem Vineyards
4. Beneduce Vineyards
5. Unionville Vineyards
6. Old York Cellars

Restaurants/Eateries:

Clinton House – Founded in 1743, this landmark restaurant exudes old-fashioned charm with its dark wood and solid stone hearth. The Clinton House offers both traditional staples like burgers and sandwiches, and less common fare like snapper turtle soup and Seafood Newburg.
Address: 2 West Main Street, Clinton, NJ
Phone: (908) 730-9300

Luna Pizza – Finding good pizza is the countryside can be a challenge, but one of the best pizzerias in the state is located in a Victorian-style house in the town of Three Bridges. Their plain pizza is thin and has a delicious sauce, but Luna is most renowned for their sausage pie.
Address: 429 Main Street, Three Bridges, NJ
Phone: (908) 284-2321

Pattenburg House – This quaint village tavern has been serving thirsty locals and travelers since 1872, and even operated as a bar during Prohibition. Besides having a wide selection of drinks, the Pattenburg House has bands every weekend, and is known for its unique pub grub.
Address: 512 Pattenburg Road (Route 614), Asbury, NJ
Phone: (908) 735-2547

Lodging:

Lambertville House Hotel – Located in the heart of downtown Lambertville, this historic hotel was built in 1812 and has lodged dignitaries, business leaders, and several US Presidents. All 26 rooms in this boutique hotel have luxury amenities such as gas fireplaces and jetted bathtubs.
Address: 32 Bridge Street, Lambertville, NJ
Phone: (888) 867-8859

Berry Preserve Bed and Breakfast – Berry Preserve is a great place to escape from the stresses of modern life. This rural retreat offers three well-decorated guest rooms, ten acres of tranquil woods, a skylit dining room, and delicious breakfasts made by the Berry family.
Address: 215 Turkey Hill Road, Asbury, NJ
Phone: (908) 479-6242

Attractions:

Red Mill Museum – Founded as a wool mill around 1810, the Red Mill is one the most famous landmarks in New Jersey, and is routinely shown in state tourism ads. This picturesque museum located on the South Branch of the Raritan River houses over 40,000 historic artifacts.
Address: 56 Main Street, Clinton, NJ
Phone: (908) 735-4101

Green Sergeant's Covered Bridge – While most covered bridges disappeared when cars replaced the horse and buggy, this one-lane wooden bridge in the Amwell Valley remains. Green Sergeant's is on the National Register of Historic Places, and is said to be haunted.
Address: Rosemont-Ringoes Road (Route 604), Stockton, NJ
Phone: N/A

Alba Vineyard

In 1980, Rudolf Marchesi planted a vineyard on a former dairy farm near the village of Finesville. The New Jersey native had grown grapes in the foothills of California, but decided that it would be more interesting to join the then-nascent Garden State wine boom. Alba Vineyard, named for the Italian word for dawn, opened two years later. Marchesi partnered with Tom Sharko who would later become the sole proprietor of Alba. Under the direction of Sharko and winemaker John Altmaier, Alba has become a New Jersey landmark.

Whether you are a novice or expert at wine tasting, a visit to Alba will be worthwhile. The winery looks like it could be located in Bordeaux, being in a 200-year-old limestone and oak structure in the picturesque Musconetcong River Valley. Alba makes a variety of white, red, and dessert wines from its own fruit, and has its Chelsea Cellars label for vintages it produces from Washington state grapes. While Alba has many good wines, my favorite is their Pinot Noir, a dry delicate red that goes very well with duck or lamb.

Address: 269 Riegelsville Warren Glen Road (Route 627), Finesville, NJ

Phone: (908) 995-7800

Website: www.albavineyard.com

E-mail: wine@albavineyard.com

Appellation: Warren Hills

Other labels: Chelsea Cellars

First vines planted: 1980

Opened to the public: 1982

Key people: Rudolph Marchesi (founder); Tom Sharko (owner); John Altmaier (winemaker)

Acres planted: 42

Cases/year: 11,000

Grapes: Barbera, Cabernet Franc, Cabernet Sauvignon, Cayuga White, Chambourcin, Chardonnay, Gewürztraminer, Malbec, Merlot, Pinot Noir, Riesling, Syrah, and Vidal Blanc

Other fruit: blueberries and raspberries

Other attractions: picnicking, weddings

Days: daily tastings, tours on weekends

Villa Milagro Vineyards

The first time I visited Villa Milagro, I was packed in a car with five friends on a cold February day, and our car got stuck in a snow bank along their long driveway. Owner Steve Gambino used a tractor to pull us out, and then his wife Audrey graciously offered us a free tasting. The family's hospitality is matched by the beauty of their vineyard, which is located on a mountaintop overlooking the Delaware River near Finesville. Villa Milagro, which is Spanish for "house of miracles," was first planted in 2003, and opened to the public four years later.

The Gambinos only make a handful of wines, but all the grapes are grown organically. In fact, this is the only organic winery in New Jersey. There is a tourist train from Phillipsburg to Villa Milagro on Saturdays and Sundays from May to October. This steam locomotive runs along the scenic Delaware River, and has a winery car which is decorated with grapevines and tea lights. Try Rosita, a semi-sweet blend of Muscat Blanc and hybrid grapes. This blush wine has slight bite and would pair well with Gouda cheese.

Address: 33 Warren Glen Road, Finesville, NJ

Phone: (908) 995-2072

Website: www.villamilagrovineyards.com

E-mail: info@villamilagrovineyards.com

Appellation: Warren Hills

First vines planted: 2003

Opened to the public: 2007

Key people: Steve & Audrey Gambino (owners)

Acres cultivated: 11

Cases/year: 1,500

Grapes: Cabernet Franc, Cabernet Sauvignon, Chardonnay, Frontenac, Muscat Blanc, Malbec, Merlot, Norton (Cynthiana), Pinot Gris, Sangiovese, Syrah, Vidal Blanc, and Villard Blanc

Other fruit: N/A

Other attractions: organic wines, picnicking, tourist train, weddings

Days: tastings and tours on weekends

Mount Salem Vineyards

Mount Salem Vineyards is different than most of the other places listed in this book in that it is a boutique winery that specializes in premium wines made from Austrian and Northern Italian grapes. Peter Leitner planted a vineyard in 2005 on historic farmland on the slopes of Mount Salem in Pittstown. He converted a 200-year-old barn into a tasting room, and in 2010, Mount Salem opened to the public. Peter advocates Burgundian winemaking practices, which entails a strong emphasis on *terroir*, the use of high-quality fruit and labor-intensive farming practices.

Mount Salem serves as a winegrowing test site for Rutgers University. It is the only winery in New Jersey that utilizes Petit Manseng, Schiava Grossa, St. Laurent, and Vespolina, which are *vinifera* grapes indigenous to mountainous regions of Western Europe. Try the Petit Manseng. Despite being a white wine made in stainless steel, it tasted like a red wine aged in oak. Peter told me that he also tasted the oakiness, and suggested pairing this enigmatic wine with ham or pate.

Address: 54 Mount Salem Road, Pittstown, NJ

Phone: 908-735-9359

Website: www.mountsalemvineyards.com

E-mail: pleitner@mountsalemvineyards.com

Appellation: N/A

First vines planted: 2005

Opened to the public: 2010

Key people: Peter Leitner (owner)

Acres cultivated: 7

Cases/year: 1,000

Grapes: Albariño, Barbera, Blaufränkisch (Lemberger), Cabernet Franc, Chardonnay, Grüner Veltliner, Merlot, Nebbiolo, Petit Manseng, Riesling, Sauvignon Blanc, Schiava Grossa, St. Laurent, Traminette, Vespolina, and Zweigelt

Other fruit used: N/A

Days: tastings on weekends and by appointment

Beneduce Vineyards

Beneduce Vineyards bubbles with youth. The winery is run by Michael Beneduce Jr. and Justen Beneduce Hiles, a 20-something brother-sister combination whose family has been farming for four generations. Mike is the winemaker and vineyard manager, and Justen is the marketing and event director. In 2000, their father, Michael Beneduce Sr. purchased a 51-acre farm in Pittstown to supply a garden center that he owned. Nine years later, a vineyard was planted, and Beneduce opened in 2012.

Beneduce (pronounced *ben-ay-doo-chay*) focuses on aromatic varietals. It is the only winery in New Jersey that produces wine from Noiret, which is a red hybrid grape developed in New York in 1973. Check out their Tropical Oasis, a greenhouse filled with fig, palm, and citrus trees that they use for events. My favorite wine was the Cabernet Franc. Aged in American oak, it burst with a complex array of flavors and then ended with a soft finish.

Address: 1 Jeremiah Lane, Pittstown, NJ

Phone: (908) 996-3823

Website: beneducevineyards.com

E-mail: justen@beneducevineyards.com

Appellation: N/A

First vines planted: 2009

Opened to the public: 2012

Key people: Michael Beneduce Sr., Michael Beneduce Jr., Justen Beneduce Hiles (owners)

Acres cultivated: 10

Cases/year: 4,000

Grapes: Blaufränkisch (Lemberger), Cabernet Franc, Cabernet Sauvignon, Chambourcin, Chardonnay, Corot Noir, Gewürztraminer, Malbec, Noiret, Pinot Noir, Riesling, and Syrah

Other fruit: N/A

Other attractions: picnicking, weddings

Days: tastings Wednesday to Sunday

Unionville Vineyards

Unionville Vineyards, located in the bucolic countryside of Hunterdon County, is one of the most renowned wineries in the state. The vineyard, named for a former village near Ringoes, was planted in 1988, and opened to the public five years later. In 2008, founders Kris Nielsen and Patricia Galloway sold Unionville to investors. Unionville's Chardonnay was the only wine from the United States to win a Gold (Best in Class) medal at the 2010 International Wine and Spirit Competition, and it was the top-rated American wine at the Judgment of Princeton.

Unionville's vintages are crafted by winemaker Cameron Stark. It is the only winery in New Jersey that produces wine from Counoise, Horizon, Marsanne, and Roussanne. Horizon is a white hybrid grape developed in New York in 1945, whereas the other three varietals are *vinifera* grapes indigenous to the Rhone River Valley of France. When I visited, I tried their famed Pheasant Hill Chardonnay, which started with explosive fruit flavors and ended with a silk-smooth finish. Pair this signature wine with delectable piece of Atlantic salmon.

Address: 9 Rocktown Road, Ringoes, NJ

Phone: (908) 788-0400

Website: unionvillevineyards.com

E-mail: sbrody@unionvillevineyards.com

Appellation: N/A

First vines planted: 1988

Opened to the public: 1993

Key people: Kris Nielsen & Patricia Galloway (founders); Zvi Eiref, John Hawkins, Lisa Hawkins, Robert Wilson (owners); Cameron Stark (winemaker)

Acres cultivated: 54

Cases/year: 8,500

Grapes: Albariño, Cabernet Franc, Cabernet Sauvignon, Cayuga White, Chambourcin, Chardonnay, Counoise, Durif, Gewürztraminer, Horizon, Marsanne, Merlot, Mourvèdre, Petit Verdot, Pinot Gris, Pinot Noir, Riesling, Roussanne, Seyval Blanc, Syrah, and Vidal Blanc and Viognier

Other fruit: N/A

Signature wine: Chardonnay

Other attractions: pet-friendly, picnicking, weddings

Days: daily tastings, tours on weekends

Old York Cellars

Some years ago while driving through the rolling hills of western New Jersey, I visited a winery named Amwell Valley Vineyard. In 1978, Michael Fisher planted French-American hybrid grapes in the Sourland Mountains near Ringoes, and Amwell Valley Vineyard sold wine from 1982 until 2005. The winery was purchased by David Wolin and reopened as Old York Cellars in 2010. The winery is named after Old York Road, a historic roadway connecting New York City and Philadelphia, and is run by winemaker Scott Gares and general manager Laurin Dorman.

Old York Cellars is the only winery in New Jersey that produces wine from Colobel, a red hybrid grape developed in France in the early twentieth century that's often used for wine coloration. They also have a separate brand of New Jersey themed vintages named What Exit Wines that are used to raise money for Hurricane Sandy relief. Old York has a small gallery featuring the works of local artists and regularly offers art classes. Try their Cabernet Sauvignon, which starts dry and soft, but ends with a bit of a spice.

Address: 80 Old York Road, Ringoes, NJ

Phone: (908) 284-9463

Website: www.oldyorkcellars.com

E-mail: info@oldyorkcellars.com

Appellation: N/A

Former name: Amwell Valley Vineyard

Other labels: What Exit Wines

First vines planted: 1978

Opened to the public: 1982 (Amwell Valley); 2010 (Old York Cellars)

Key people: David Wolin (owner); Scott Gares (winemaker); Laurin Dorman (general manager)

Acres cultivated: 12

Cases/year: 3,600

Grapes: Barbera, Cabernet Sauvignon, Cayuga White, Chardonnay, Chenin Blanc, Colobel, Landot Noir, Malbec, Marechal Foch, Merlot, Pinot Gris, Riesling, Seyval Blanc, Syrah, Vidal Blanc, and Vignoles

Other fruit: blackberries and peaches

Other attractions: art gallery, picnicking, weddings

Days: daily tastings, tours on weekends

Central Jersey is often forgotten when it comes to winemaking. There is no viticultural area or winegrowing organization specifically for this area. Until the last decade, Cream Ridge was the only winery in this region. However, Monmouth, Mercer, and Ocean counties have both a rich agricultural tradition and quick access to the Garden State Parkway and New Jersey Turnpike, and so it's no surprise that more wineries have opened here. If one word could describe the winemaking of the region, it would be diversity.

Central Jersey's wineries offer high quality vintages and an eagerness to experiment. In other parts of the state, I find that many of the winemakers come from families that always grew grapes and made wine for personal consumption. Here that's not the case, and I feel that the lack of familial background has forced them to learn good winemaking technique and granted them the freedom to make wines that others wouldn't consider. For example, Laurita makes several wines using milk, and Cream Ridge has an espresso-based wine.

The region is blessed with rich dark soil, and a climate that's intermediate between Northern and Southern Jersey. Central Jersey vineyards grow both *vinifera* and hybrid grapes. While these wineries definitely cannot grow grapes like Tempranillo or Malvasia, Chardonnays and Pinot Grigios are common here. Although these counties are becoming increasingly suburbanized, there is still a large amount of open land in this area, and I could envision more Central Jersey wineries opening in the next few years.

The Central Jersey road trip is probably the most challenging one in this book. While the entire wine trail is only 72 miles start to finish, it involves driving on nearly 35 different roads. Get a GPS, or be really good at reading maps. That being said, this trip offers the greatest variety of wineries. Terhune is a well-known produce farm that recently began selling wine, Laurita has a massive winery complex with an accompanying bed and breakfast and equestrian center, and Peppadew Fresh is a residence with a barn converted into a tasting room.

Road Trip #3

Wineries:

1. Peppadew Fresh Vineyards
2. Four JG's Orchards & Vineyards
3. Laurita Winery
4. Cream Ridge Winery
5. Working Dog Winery
6. Terhune Orchards
7. Hopewell Valley Vineyards

Restaurants/Eateries:

De Lorenzo's Tomato Pies – Founded in Trenton in 1947, this beloved pizzeria is now located in Robbinsville. De Lorenzo's makes an amazing pizza with a very thin crust and a delicious sauce, and the Star-Ledger's Munchmobile rated their sausage pizza as the best in the Garden State.
Address: 2350 U.S. Highway 33, Robbinsville, NJ
Phone: (609) 341-8480

Plumsted Grill – Does having a good food in a rustic setting appeal to you? This tavern in a log cabin has deer antler chandeliers and brick fireplaces, and is frequented by bikers, professionals, and many other types. Their burgers and sandwiches are top notch.
Address: 457 Pinehurst Road (Route 539), Cream Ridge, NJ
Phone: (609) 758-5552

Colts Neck Inn Steak & Chop House – The Colts Neck Inn has been a watering hole since 1717. During the American Revolution, it was a meeting place for local minutemen, and Laird once distilled their applejack there. Today, this landmark is renowned for its steaks.
Address: 6 Route 537 West, Colts Neck, NJ
Phone: (732) 462-0383

Lodging:

Molly Pitcher Inn – Named for the legendary hero of the Battle of Monmouth, this renowned hotel overlooks the scenic Navesink River. Besides providing luxury accommodations, the Molly Pitcher Inn offers a top-shelf American restaurant and access to cosmopolitan Red Bank.
Address: 88 Riverside Avenue, Red Bank, NJ
Phone: (732) 747-2500

Inn at Glencairn – This Georgian manor house was built in 1736 by Dutch settlers. The Inn at Glencairn combines eighteenth century woodwork and a 12-foot-wide colonial era fireplaces with central air conditioning, flat screen TVs, and high speed internet.
Address: 3301 Lawrenceville Road (Route 206), Princeton, NJ
Phone: (609) 497-1737

Attractions:

Stone Pony – Founded in 1973, this legendary nightclub was an early stomping ground for Bruce Springsteen, Jon Bon Jovi, and Southside Johnny. Located next to the Asbury Park Boardwalk, the Stone Pony has performers on most Friday and Saturday evenings.
Address: 913 Ocean Avenue, Asbury Park, NJ
Phone: (732) 502-0600

Princeton Battlefield State Park – In 1777, Washington defeated the British at Princeton. Besides marking the battlefield, this 210-acre park has a museum of military artifacts and a stone memorial for the 21 British and 15 American soldiers who died there.
Address: 500 Mercer Road (Route 583), Princeton, NJ
Phone: (609) 921-0074

Peppadew Fresh Vineyards

There is only one place in the United States that grows peppadews, a sharply-flavored pepper from South Africa that looks like a cherry tomato. That same farm also grows grapes and produces wine. Pierre Crawley bought a flower farm in Morganville, and in 2008 planted peppadews. In 2011, grapes were cultivated, and a year later the winery opened to the public. The United States Department of Agriculture awarded the farm $260,000 to expand peppadew production and distribution.

At the current time, Peppadew Fresh only offers a handful of wines, but it is one of my favorite vineyards to visit. Pierre is very knowledgeable about the wine industry, and makes visitors feel as though they are at home. The tasting room is in a nineteenth century barn that was renovated to include modern heating, café-style tables, and big screen TVs. Outside is a fire pit and patio seating. I suggest getting a glass of their Chambourcin, sitting down, and enjoying the day conversing to Pierre.

Address: 97 Harbor Road, Morganville, NJ

Phone: (908) 507-2240

Website: peppadewfreshvineyards.com

E-mail: pierre@peppadewusa.com

Appellation: N/A

First vines planted: 2011

Opened to the public: 2012

Key people: Pierre Crawley (owner)

Acres cultivated: 4

Cases/year: 900

Grapes: Cabernet Franc, Cabernet Sauvignon, Chambourcin, Chardonnay, Pinot Gris, Pinot Noir, and Riesling

Other fruit: N/A

Other attractions: pet-friendly, picnicking, weddings

Other products: azaleas, flowering quinces, hydrangeas, peppadews, pussywillows

Days: tastings on weekends

.

Four JG's Orchards & Vineyards

As you drive pass the bucolic horse farms of Colts Neck, you will come upon a large vineyard on a hill. Named for the shared initials of John and Janet Giunco, and their children Jill and John Jr., Four JG's was first planted in 1999, and their tasting room opened to the public in 2004. Four JG's sells grapes to other New Jersey wineries, and was instrumental in establishing an on-campus vineyard and winemaking program at Monmouth University.

The winery is located in a historic farming area, and some of the buildings on the farm date back to the eighteenth century. The winery is only open on select weekends, so call in advance. I strongly recommend their Monmouth Blush, an off-dry blend of Vidal Blanc and Cabernet Franc that would go well at a picnic. Four JG's also offers a frozen slushy made from Monmouth Blush, and often serves apple cider doughnuts from Delicious Orchards, a local farm market.

Address: 127 Hillsdale Road, Colts Neck, NJ

Phone: (908) 930-8066

Website: www.4jgswinery.com

E-mail: cnvintner@optonline.net

Appellation: N/A

First vines planted: 1999

Opened to the public: 2004

Key people: John & Janet Giunco, Jill Giunco, John Giunco Jr. (owners)

Acres cultivated: 40

Cases/year: 2,500

Grapes: Cabernet Franc, Cayuga White, Chambourcin, Chardonnay, Vidal Blanc, and Vignoles (Ravat 51)

Other fruit: N/A

Days: tastings on select weekends

Laurita Winery

When you think of a New Jersey winery, do you think of a 20,000 square foot building on the top of a hill that not only serves wine to hundreds of people at a time but also has a bistro, and is connected to a bed and breakfast and equestrian center? If not, you haven't been to Laurita Winery. Ray Shea and Randy Johnson purchased a horse farm and two abandoned dairy farms in New Egypt, and in 1998 planted grapes. Named after Randy's mother Laura and Ray's mother Rita, the Inn at Laurita opened in 2002 and the winery opened six years later.

Laurita's vintages are made by famed winemaker Nicholaas Opdam. The winery produces both traditional *vinifera* wines such as Albariño and Zweigelt, and also fun blends like Windswept White and Tailgate Red. Laurita produces a fruit wine from strawberries and milk, and a dessert wine using milk, chocolate, and Chambourcin grapes, making it the only Garden State winery to have dairy-based wines. My favorite wine was the Lemberger, which was dry and smooth, and would pair nicely with a duck dinner.

Address: 85 Archertown Road, New Egypt, NJ

Phone: (609) 752-0200

Website: www.lauritawinery.com

E-mail: manager@lauritawinery.com

Appellation: Outer Coastal Plain

First vines planted: 1998

Opened to the public: 2008

Key people: Randy Johnson, Ray Shea (owners); Nicolaas Opdam (winemaker)

Acres cultivated: 44

Cases/year: 14,000

Grapes: Albariño, Blaufränkisch (Lemberger), Cabernet Franc, Cabernet Sauvignon, Chambourcin, Chardonnay, Grenache, Merlot, Norton (Cynthiana), Pinot Gris, and Zweigelt

Other fruit: strawberries

Other attractions: bed and breakfast, bistro, horseback riding, and weddings

Days: tastings Wednesday to Sunday

Cream Ridge Winery

Tom Amabile made wine as a hobby, and he had a particular interest in cherry wine. In 1987, he and wife Joan planted grapes near the village of Cream Ridge, and a year later, Cream Ridge Winery had its debut. Since then, their Ciliegia Amabile (cherry wine) has won the Governor's Cup four times for best fruit wine in the state. I am sad to report that Tom passed away in early 2014, but his winemaking tradition lives on at Cream Ridge. Today, the winery is run by his son Jerry, and his business partners Tim and Jackie Schlitzer.

Cream Ridge has a wide selection of wines, and they frequently experiment with new varieties. They are the only winery in the state to use apricots or coffee to make wine. Java Berry is a blackberry wine infused with espresso, and this caffeinated concoction has the aroma of a fresh cup of coffee and the sweetness of a dessert wine. I recommend their Petite Sirah which is initially dry, but ends with a spicy kick.

Address: 145 Allentown Davis Station Rd (Route 539), Cream Ridge, NJ

Phone: (609) 259-9797

Website: www.creamridgewinery.com

E-mail: crwinery@creamridgewinery.com

Appellation: N/A

First vines planted: 1987

Opened to the public: 1988

Key people: Tom & Joan Amabile (founders); Jerry Amabile, Tim & Jackie Schlitzer (managers)

Acres cultivated: 14

Cases/year: 5,000

Grapes: Barbera, Cabernet Franc, Cabernet Sauvignon, Chambourcin, Chardonnay, Durif (Petite Sirah), Fredonia, Merlot, Muscat Blanc, Niagara, Pinot Gris, Pinot Noir, Riesling, Sangiovese, Sauvignon Blanc, Syrah, Vidal Blanc, and Zinfandel

Other fruit: almonds, apricots, blackberries, black currants, blueberries, cherries, cranberries, kiwi, limes, mangoes, pineapples, and raspberries

Signature wine: Ciliegia Amabile (cherry wine)

Other attractions: pet-friendly

Days: daily tastings

Working Dog Winery

Most wineries in New Jersey are owned by one or two families. However, in 2001 a group of friends planted grapes on farmland near the border of Robbinsville and East Windsor. Silver Decoy Winery, which is named after one of the owners known for his silver hair and hunting prowess, open two years later. The winery changed it name in 2013 because of a large California winery with a similar brand name, but five of the friends still operate the vineyard.

Not surprisingly, this winery has many dog-themed fundraisers, and a number of working dogs make this farm their home. At least one of the owners is usually on site, and they are quite personable. Working Dog Winery has a large covered patio where you can sit back, sip some wine, and get a spectacular view of the vineyard. I strongly recommend the aptly-named Retriever wine, a Bordeaux-style red made from Cabernet Sauvignon, Syrah, and Merlot, and which pairs well with filet mignon.

Address: 610 Windsor-Perrineville Road, East Windsor, NJ

Phone: (609) 371-6000

Website: www.workingdogwinerynj.com

E-mail: info@workingdogwinerynj.com

Appellation: N/A

Former name: Silver Decoy Winery

First vines planted: 2001

Opened to the public: 2003

Key people: Todd Abrahams, Brian Carduner, Mark Carduner, Russell Forman, Jerry Watlington (owners)

Acres cultivated: 16

Cases/year: 3,500

Grapes: Cabernet Franc, Chambourcin, Chardonnay, Marechal Foch, Merlot, Pinot Gris, Riesling, Sangiovese, Syrah, Traminette, and Viognier

Other fruit: blueberries

Other attractions: pet-friendly, picnicking, weddings

Days: tastings Friday to Sunday

Terhune Orchards

After serving in the Peace Corps, Gary and Pam Mount bought a farm from the Terhune family in 1975. The Mounts tripled the size of the Lawrence Township farm, which over time has become famous for its fresh produce and baked goods. Upon returning home after living in San Francisco for six years, their daughter Tannwen suggested that the family become winemakers. In 2003 grapes were planted, and Terhune Orchards began selling wine in 2010.

The tasting room is in a converted barn, and wine is also sold by the bottle in their farm store. When I visited, I talked to Gary who is very knowledgeable about winegrowing. This is the only New Jersey winery that produces Chardonel, a white hybrid of Chardonnay and Seyval Blanc developed in New York in 1953. Just Peachy won the New Jersey Governor's Cup for fruit wines in 2013. This blend of peaches and apples tasted like apple cider, but not as sweet and with a very smooth finish. Pair this delectable wine with a piece of homemade apple pie.

Address: 330 Cold Soil Road, Princeton, NJ

Phone: (609) 924-2310

Website: www.terhuneorchards.com

E-mail: info@terhuneorchards.com

Appellation: N/A

First vines planted: 2003

Opened to the public: 2010

Key people: Gary & Pam Mount, Tannwen Mount (owners)

Acres cultivated: 5

Cases/year: 1,100

Grapes: Cabernet Franc, Cabernet Sauvignon, Chambourcin, Chardonel, Chardonnay, Muscat Ottenell, Niagara, Pinot Gris, Riesling, Sauvignon Blanc, Traminette, and Vidal Blanc

Other fruit: apples, blueberries, and peaches

Other attractions: fruit picking, picnicking, wagon rides

Other products: bread, cider, doughnuts, flowers, fruits, herbs, pies, vegetables

Days: tastings Thursday to Sunday, bottle sales every day

Hopewell Valley Vineyards

Sergio and Violetta Neri have winemaking in their blood. He comes from a line of Tuscan vintners who made Brunello di Montalcino wines, and her grandmother made traditional Macedonian Greek white wines. In 2001, the couple planted grapes in the quaint town of Hopewell, and two years later Hopewell Valley Vineyards began selling wine. I first visited soon after they opened, and the two things that stood out were the owners' friendliness and a selection of uncommon vintages.

The tasting room looks like a jazz club, with its artwork, piano, and bistro-style chairs and table. It is the only winery in New Jersey that used Brachetto, a red *vinifera* grape indigenous to the Piedmont region of Italy that is often used to make sparkling wines. To add to the charm, Hopewell Valley sells brick oven pizzas, and makes olive oil from olives grown in Tuscany. Try their White Merlot, a unique wine which has the delicacy of a Pinot Grigio, the complexity of a Cabernet Franc, and sweetness of a Concord.

Address: 46 Yard Road, Pennington, NJ

Phone: (609) 737-4465

Website: hopewellvalleyvineyards.com

E-mail: violetta@hopewellvalleyvineyards.com

Appellation: N/A

First vines planted: 2001

Opened to the public: 2003

Key people: Sergio & Violetta Neri (owners)

Acres cultivated: 25

Cases/year: 6,000

Grapes: Barbera, Brachetto, Cabernet Sauvignon, Chambourcin, Chardonnay, Merlot, Muscat Blanc, Pinot Gris, Sangiovese, and Vidal Blanc

Other fruit: N/A

Other attractions: pet-friendly, picnicking, weddings

Other products: olive oil, pizza

Days: daily tastings

Introduction to the Southern Shore

The Southern Shore region consists of Atlantic and Cape May counties. While best known for famous beach resort towns like Atlantic City, Wildwood, and Cape May, the area also has hundreds of thousands of acres of pine forests interspersed with small farms. The climate of this region is similar to that of the winegrowing regions of France and Italy, and the acidic soil of the Pine Barrens is perfect for grapes. The area near Egg Harbor City has had vineyards since the 1860s, and in recent years Hammonton has become the epicenter of New Jersey wine production.

All of the wineries in this region are part of the Outer Coastal Plain Viticultural Area, which includes most of South Jersey. Because the Southern Shore has warmers winters than other parts of New Jersey, it's possible to grow Southern European *vinifera* varieties like Dolcetto or Tempranillo. Fruit wines are big business here, often made from locally-grown blackberries, blueberries, cranberries, and peaches, but also including more exotic crops such as beach plums and huckleberries. Most of these wineries are members of the Garden State Wine Growers Association.

I break this region into two road trips. The first seven wineries are in Atlantic County. Although I do not have a favorite winery, this is my favorite wine trail, and nobody that I have taken to these wineries has been disappointed. The Atlantic County wineries are the largest and oldest in the state, but at the same time they are all family-owned and give very personal service. While all the road trips in the book are scenic, this one is the most likely to make you feel as though you are in the French or Italian countryside.

The remaining six wineries are in Cape May County. Just fifteen years ago, Cape May County was a non-entity in the winery world which is surprising considering its good climate and soil. With easy access from the shore towns, today this is the most popular wine trail in the state. In order to avoid tourist crowds, visit when they first open in the morning or during the off-season. At the time of this book's writing, the Cape May wineries are trying to get the federal government to recognize a new viticultural area known as the Cape May Peninsula AVA.

Road Trip #4

Wineries:

1. Balic Winery
2. Bellview Winery
3. DiMatteo Vineyards
4. Plagido's Winery
5. Tomasello Winery
6. Sylvin Farms Winery
7. Renault Winery

Restaurants/Eateries:

Angelo's Fairmount Tavern – Many Atlantic City restaurants are overpriced or geared towards gamblers, but this 80-year old landmark is a definite exception. Angelo's offers traditional Italian food, very cozy dining rooms, and walls covered with decades of baseball paraphernalia.
Address: 2300 Fairmount Avenue, Atlantic City, NJ
Phone: (609) 344-2439

Ye Olde Mill Street Pub – This is a traditional English-style pub – dimly lit, quaint, and cozy. They have a wide selection of beers and wine, and their sandwiches and burgers are outstanding. Before winery hopping through Atlantic County, I always stop here for lunch.
Address: 6033 Main Street, Mays Landing, NJ
Phone: (609) 625-2466

Kelsey & Kim's Southern Café – If you like traditional southern cuisine, pay a visit to Kelsey and Kim's. Serving both breakfast and dinner, this BYOB is all about comfort food. The owner and manager are quite personable, and prices are very reasonable.
Address: 201 Melrose Avenue, Atlantic City, NJ
Phone: (609) 350-6800

Lodging:

Inn at Sugar Hill – This historic bed and breakfast overlooks the scenic Great Egg Harbor River since 1845. Most of the rooms have a fireplace, and the inn serves breakfast, lunch, dinner. Somewhat unusual for B&B, The Inn at Sugar Hill has a tavern with live music on the weekend.
Address: 5704 Somers Point Mays Landing Road, Mays Landing, NJ
Phone: (609) 625-2226

Tuscany House Hotel – After you've visited all seven wineries on this road trip, and you are in no condition to operate a motor vehicle, stay at this lovely hotel connected to Renault Winery. The Italian villa architecture is amazing, and all fifty rooms in this hotel are unique.
Address: 72 Bremen Avenue, Egg Harbor City, NJ
Phone: (609) 965-2111

Attractions:

Lucy the Elephant –Mention the town of Margate, and the first thing that come to mind is Lucy. Built in 1881, this six-story tin and wood elephant-shaped structure is a historic landmark. Lucy can be climbed, and there is a howdah at top where visitors can sit.
Address: 9200 Atlantic Avenue, Margate, NJ
Phone: (609) 823-6473

Saint Padre Pio Shrine – Located in Buena near Bellview Winery, this outdoor Roman Catholic shrine dedicated to twentieth-century Italian saint Padre Pio was built by local farmers. Believers attest that aliments have been cured by praying at this shrine.
Address: Corner of Harding Highway (Route 40), Central Avenue, and Weymouth Road (Route 690) in Landisville, NJ
Phone: N/A

Balic Winery

Balic is in Mays Landing, a town of Victorian houses, pine forests, and small farms, a half-hour west of Atlantic City. Savo Balić had operated a vineyard in Yugoslavia near the Adriatic Sea. He came to New Jersey, and in 1966 opened the winery. The land has a long history of grape cultivation – the vineyard was first planted in the early 1800s by descendants of the original settlers of Mays Landing. Balić's nephew, Bojan Boskovic, immigrated to the United States in 1993 to work for his uncle, and has since taken over the winery.

It is the only winery in New Jersey that produces wine from Vranec, a red grape that is indigenous to Montenegro. They are also the only producers of huckleberry wine in the Garden State. Their signature wine is pomegranate, and they advertise the medicinal benefits from the fruit's antioxidants. The pomegranate wine has an intense purple color, an amazing sweet and sour flavor, and a crisp finish. This wine could be paired with any dessert, or could be used as an after-dinner sipping wine.

Address: 6623 Harding Highway (Route 40), Mays Landing, NJ

Phone: (609) 625-2166

Website: www.balicwinery.com

E-mail: info@balicwinery.com

Appellation: Outer Coastal Plain

First vines planted: Early 1800s

Opened to the public: 1966

Key people: Savo Balić (founder); Bojan Boskovic (owner)

Acres cultivated: 57

Cases/year: undisclosed

Grapes: Cabernet Franc, Cabernet Sauvignon, Chambourcin, Chardonnay, Chenin Blanc, Pinot Noir, Riesling, Sangiovese, Vidal Blanc, Viognier, Vranac, and Zinfandel

Other fruit: almonds, blackberries, blueberries, cherries, cranberries, huckleberries, mangoes, pomegranates, raspberries, and strawberries

Signature wine: pomegranate

Days: daily tastings

Bellview Winery

Jim Quarella has long been at the forefront of farming innovation. Jim's great-grandfather Angelo immigrated from Italy and in 1914 started a fruit and vegetable farm in Landisville. In order to compete with global competition in the produce market, Jim planted specialty Asian vegetables in the early 1990s. He's been growing wine grapes since age 16. A full-scale vineyard was planted in 2000, and the following year the winery opened. The name Bellview is of Italian origin, but the family isn't sure if it's named for a specific place in Italy.

They are one of only a handful of wineries in the United States that produces wine from dandelions, and the only winery in New Jersey to use Tinta Cao and Touriga Nacional, which are red *vinifera* grapes indigenous to Portugal. I strongly recommend both the Black Currant and Dandelion wines. Black Currant was smooth and effervesced with the sweetness of fruit. Dandelion is based on an old family recipe, and was just as sweet and smooth as Black Currant, but with an herbal kick.

Address: 150 Atlantic Street, Landisville, NJ

Phone: (856) 697-7172

Website: www.bellviewwinery.com

E-mail: info@bellviewwinery.com

Appellation: Outer Coastal Plain

First vines planted: 2000

Opened to the public: 2001

Key people: Jim Quarella (owner)

Acres cultivated: 40

Cases/year: 8,000

Grapes: Blaufränkisch (Lemberger), Cabernet Franc, Cabernet Sauvignon, Cayuga White, Chambourcin, Chardonnay, Fredonia, Ives Noir, Merlot, Muscat Ottonel, Niagara, Petit Verdot, Pinot Gris, Syrah, Tinta Cão, Touriga Nacional, Traminette, Vidal Blanc, and Viognier

Other fruit: black currants, blueberries, cranberries, and dandelions

Other attractions: pet-friendly, picnicking, weddings

Days: daily tastings

DiMatteo Vineyards

DiMatteo Vineyards is the quintessence of a family-run business. Each time I visit their tasting room, or taste their wine at a festival, a member of the family is present. Like many families, they have long made wine for personal consumption. In 2000, Frank DiMatteo Jr. and Frank DiMatteo III planted a vineyard in Hammonton, and two years later, the winery opened. Frank Jr. runs the tasting room like an old-school host – women get served before men. Frank III is a lifetime farmer, and is usually in the fields meticulously tending to his vines.

In 2010, the winery moved across town to a much larger facility. DiMatteo specializes in making wine from often-snubbed native varieties such as Concord and Ives, and they are the only winery in the state growing Diamond grapes, which are a Concord-based hybrid developed in the 1880s. My favorite vintage is their award-winning Pasquale Red. This wine is highly satisfying product of old-fashioned Italian winemaking crossed with indigenous American grapes, and would be a great compliment for a pasta dinner.

Address: 951 8th Street, Hammonton, NJ

Phone: (609) 704-1414

Website: www.dimatteowinery.net

E-mail: dimatteowine@wildblue.net

Appellation: Outer Coastal Plain

First vines planted: 2000

Opened to the public: 2002

Moved to new location: 2010

Key people: Frank DiMatteo Jr., Frank DiMatteo III (owners)

Acres cultivated: 14

Cases/year: 1,500

Grapes: Cabernet Franc, Cayuga White, Chambourcin, Chancellor, Chardonnay, Concord, Diamond, Ives Noir, Merlot, Niagara, Syrah, Traminette, and Vidal Blanc

Other fruit: apples, blueberries, cranberries, peaches, pumpkins, and strawberries

Signature wine: Pasquale Red

Days: tastings Friday to Tuesday

Plagido's Winery

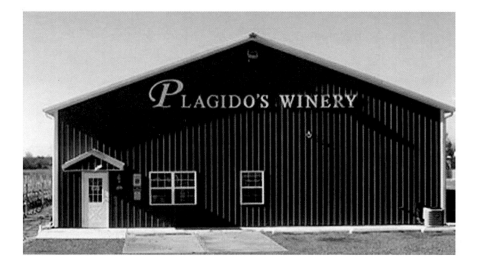

I first visited Plagido's Winery in August 2007, a week after it open to the public. I met the owner Ollie Tomasello (no relation to Tomasello Winery) who is quite down to earth and bubbles with friendliness. The winery is named for his great-grandfather Placido who immigrated from Italy in the late 1800s and started a farm in Hammonton. The family had always grown a small patch of grapes that they used to make wine for personal consumption, and in 1999, Ollie and his father, Ollie Sr., decided to become commercial winemakers.

Unlike most of the state's wineries which do better with fruit wines and white wines, Plagido has mastered the reds. It's the only New Jersey grower of Marquis grapes, a seedless white hybrid developed in New York state in 1968, which has the fruity flavor of a Chardonnay, but the crispness of a Pinot Grigio. When you visit, try the Empire wine. Strong-bodied but as smooth as silk, this after-dinner sipping wine is among the best red wines that I have ever tasted.

Address: 570 North 1st Road, Hammonton, NJ

Phone: (609) 567-4633

Website: www.plagidoswinery.com

E-mail: ollie@plagidoswinery.com

Appellation: Outer Coastal Plain

First vines planted: 1999

Opened to the public: 2007

Key people: Ollie Tomasello Sr. (founder); Ollie Tomasello Jr. (owner); Candice Francisco (general manager)

Acres cultivated: 14

Cases/year: 4,200

Grapes: Cabernet Franc, Cabernet Sauvignon, Chambourcin, Chardonnay, Concord, Fredonia, Marquis, Merlot, Niagara, and Syrah

Other fruit: apples, blackberries, blueberries, and cranberries

Days: daily tastings

Tomasello Winery

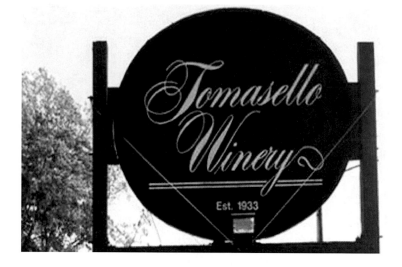

Tomasello Winery, founded in 1933, is the second-oldest winery in New Jersey. Frank Tomasello mostly grew sweet potatoes and berries, but the grapes had been grown on the family farm in Hammonton since 1888. Upon the end of Prohibition, he saw opportunity, and drove to Washington D.C. to obtain a federal winery license. For most of its history, Tomasello primarily sold dessert and sparkling wines made from native grapes (e.g., Niagara). Starting in the 1970s, the family began planting French hybrid grapes.

The winery is currently owned by Jack and Charlie Tomasello, the grandsons of its founder, and is one of the largest wineries in the state. They sell over forty different types of wine, and Tomasello has something available for every type of wine drinker. I love their Vidal Blanc Ice Wine, which is extraordinarily smooth, and bursts with fruit flavors. This after-dinner treat deserves to be paired with the richest piece of chocolate cake.

Address: 225 North White Horse Pike (Route 30), Hammonton, NJ

Phone: (609) 561-0567

Website: www.tomasellowinery.com

E-mail: wine@tomasellowinery.com

Appellation: Outer Coastal Plain

First vines planted: 1888

Opened to the public: 1933

Key people: Frank Tomasello (founder); Charlie Tomasello, Jack Tomasello (owners)

Acres cultivated: 70

Cases/year: 65,000

Grapes: Baco Noir, Cabernet Franc, Cabernet Sauvignon, Catawba, Chambourcin, Chardonnay, Colombard, Concord, De Chaunac, Landot Noir, Merlot, Muscat Blanc, Niagara, Noah, Petit Verdot, Pinot Gris, Pinot Noir, Riesling, Rkatsiteli, Sangiovese, Seyval Blanc, Syrah, Vidal Blanc, Villard Blanc, and Villard Noir

Other fruit: almonds, apples, blackberries, blueberries, cherries, cranberries, pomegranates, and raspberries

Other attractions: pet-friendly, picnicking, weddings

Days: daily tastings

Sylvin Farms Winery

Dr. Franklin Salek is a pioneer in the growing of *vinifera* grapes. Until the late 1970s, there were only a handful of wineries in the state, and they mostly produced sparkling wines or dessert wines. Grapes were planted in Germania in 1977, and eight years later the winery opened. Frank defied advice from established winemakers and took the very bold step of exclusively growing European grapes. As a result, the winery has on six occasions won the New Jersey Governor's Cup.

Sylvin Farms is located in the New Jersey Pine Barrens, and is blessed with a warm maritime breeze and gravelly loam soil. The winery's is named after both his wife Sylvia and the rustic sylvan surroundings. This is the only New Jersey winery that uses Corvina and Pinot Blanc, the former being a Venetian red grape, whereas the latter is an Alsatian white grape. Frank offers a 90-minute lecture that includes a generous amount of both knowledge and wine. Try his Cabernet Franc, which bursts with tannins but is as smooth as silk, and goes perfectly with filet mignon.

Address: 24 North Vienna Avenue, Egg Harbor City, NJ

Phone: (609) 965-1548

Website: www.sylvinfarmswinery.com

E-mail: sylvinfarms@comcast.net

Appellation: Outer Coastal Plain

First vines planted: 1977

Opened to the public: 1985

Key people: Frank Salek (owner)

Acres cultivated: 11

Cases/year: 1,000

Grapes: Barbera, Cabernet Franc, Cabernet Sauvignon, Chardonnay, Corvina, Dolcetto, Merlot, Muscat Ottonel, Nebbiolo, Pinot Blanc, Pinot Gris, Pinot Noir, Riesling, Rkatsiteli, Sangiovese, Sauvignon Blanc, Sémillon, Syrah, Tempranillo, Viognier, and Zinfandel

Other fruit: N/A

Days: wine lecture / tasting by appointment

Renault Winery

Renault is the oldest and best-known winery in New Jersey. The winery has a long and colorful history, and in recent years has blossomed into a full-fledged resort with two restaurants, a 50-room hotel, and an 18-hole golf course. In 1864, Louis Nicholas Renault planted a vineyard in Egg Harbor City using *vinifera* grapes from Europe. Renault Winery (pronounced *re-nalt*) started selling wine in 1870, and was known for their champagne. During Prohibition, the winery obtained a permit from the federal government to make sacramental and medicinal wines.

In 1977, newspaper publisher Joseph Milza purchased Renault, and began the transformation of the winery into a winery resort. Renault gives a highly informative 40-minute tour and tasting. During the tour, our guide showed us Renault's extensive collection of wineglass art and antique winemaking tools. They are the only winery in the United States to make a blueberry champagne. The American Port was the best wine that I tasted there. Made from Merlot, Cabernet Franc, and Cabernet Sauvignon, the port was strong, smooth, and sweet.

Location: 72 North Bremen Avenue, Egg Harbor City, NJ

Phone: (609) 965-2111

Website: www.renaultwinery.com

E-mail: info@renaultwinery.com

Appellation: Outer Coastal Plain

First vines planted: 1864

Opened to the public: 1870

Key people: Louis Nicolas Renault (founder); Joseph Milza (owner); Marco Bucchi (winemaker)

Acres cultivated: 48

Cases/year: 20,000

Grapes: Baco Noir, Cabernet Franc, Cabernet Sauvignon, Cayuga White, Chardonnay, Merlot, Noah, Norton (Cynthiana), Petit Verdot, Pinot Gris, Pinot Noir, Riesling, Sangiovese, Sauvignon Blanc, Vidal Blanc

Other fruit: blueberries

Other attractions: golf course, hotel, two restaurants, weddings

Days: daily tastings and tours

Road Trip #5

Wineries:

1. Natali Winery
2. Jessie Creek Winery
3. Hawk Haven Vineyard & Winery
4. Cape May Winery & Vineyard
5. Turdo Vineyards & Winery
6. Willow Creek Winery

Restaurants/Eateries:

Menz Restaurant & Bar – This unique restaurant specializes in traditional New Jersey cuisine. All the food is homemade, and many of the vegetables are from local farms. Even the drinks have a local theme, such as a peach daiquiri made with Jersey peaches.
Address: 985 South Delsea Drive (Route 47), Rio Grande, NJ
Phone: (609) 886-9500

Godmothers Restaurant – The first New Jersey wine that I ever consumed was at Godmothers. This Cape May favorite offers both basic Italian dishes like spaghetti and meatballs, as well as more upscale selections such as Trofie Fra Diavolo.
Address: 413 South Broadway, Cape May, NJ
Phone: (609) 884-4543

Lighthouse Pointe Restaurant & Bar – Some of the best seafood you can find in Cape May County is at Lighthouse Pointe. Located right outside of Wildwood on Shawcrest Island, this restaurant offers both waterfront dining and indoor seating. Their crab bisque soup is amazing.
Address: 5100 Shawcrest Road, Wildwood, NJ
Phone: (609) 522-7447

Lodging:

Gingerbread House – There are a lot of bed and breakfasts in Cape May, but the Gingerbread House is one of most attractive and best rated. Build in carpenter gothic style, this house was designed by architect Stephen Decatur Button, and is located in the heart of the historic district.
Address: 28 Gurney Street, Cape May, NJ
Phone: (609) 884-0211

Caribbean Motel – Wildwood is known for its doo-wop themed motels. This ultra-retro landmark offers 1950s-era architectural elements like a levitating ramp, canted glass walls, and recessed spaceship lights, but also has modern amenities like flat-screen TVs and free WiFi.
Address: 5600 Ocean Avenue, Wildwood Crest, NJ
Phone: (609) 522-8292

Attractions:

Hereford Inlet Lighthouse – This picturesque beacon is the only lighthouse of the Stick Style on the East Coast. After touring Hereford, walk through the adjacent Victorian gardens with its hidden benches and meandering paths that lead to the North Wildwood beach.
Address: 111 North Central Avenue, North Wildwood, NJ
Phone: (609) 522-4520

Cold Spring Village – This re-created historic village offers an image of life in Cape May County in the early nineteenth century. The volunteers who work here are very knowledgeable about local history, and Cold Spring seems more authentic and less touristy than other replica villages.
Address: 720 Shore Road (Route 9), Cape May, NJ
Phone: (609) 898-2300

Natali Vineyards

Al Natali planted a vineyard in 2001 on a former horse pasture. Natali partnered with Ray Pensari and Tony Antonelli, and they opened a tasting room six years later. The winery backs on the Delaware Bay near the village of Goshen. Upon entering the property, you will see a wooden pirate statute and a patio with chairs, tables, and tents that the winery uses for events during the summer. The tasting room is small and rustic, and looks like the inside of a house.

Usually when I visit, one of the owners is present, and they remind me of bartenders at a country pub who make everyone feel at home. A few of Natali's wines are rare – nobody else in New Jersey sells pineapple wine or banana wine. Furthermore, they are the only winery in the world known to produce wine from beach plums, a fruit that grows wild in coastal areas and is often used to make jams. I strongly recommend the banana wine which was smooth, sweet, and had the aroma of bananas, but in no way tasted like bananas.

Address: 221 N. Delsea Drive (Route 47), Cape May Court House, NJ

Phone: (609) 465-0075

Website: www.natalivineyards.com

E-mail: natalivineyards@gmail.com

Appellation: Outer Coastal Plain

First vines planted: 2001

Opened to the public: 2007

Key people: Tony Antonelli, Al Natali, Ray Pensari (owners)

Acres cultivated: 7

Cases/year: 1,800

Grapes: Cabernet Franc, Cabernet Sauvignon, Chardonnay, Dolcetto, Merlot, Muscat Blanc, Nebbiolo, Pinot Gris, Sauvignon Blanc, Syrah, Tempranillo, Trebbiano, Viognier, and Zinfandel

Other fruit: bananas, beach plums, blackberries, blueberries, cherries, cranberries, peaches, pineapples, plums, and strawberries

Other attractions: pet-friendly, picnicking, weddings

Days: daily tastings, tours by appointment

Jessie Creek Winery

The vineyard was planted in 2002 by Joseph Yuzzi. He named it Jessie Creek Vineyards, a tribute to his mother whose first name was Jessie, and the town of Dias Creek where the winery is located. Five years later, the vineyard and accompanying farmhouse was purchased by Art Reale, Bruce Morrison, and Juan Fernandez. They converted the 1846 farmhouse into a bed and breakfast which opened in 2010. Two years later, Jessie Creek Winery had its debut.

I was struck by the serenity and beauty of the winery. There are rows of well-tended grape vines, and big shady trees with picnic benches underneath. The tasting room has a veranda on the back where one could sit back and enjoy the summer day while sipping a glass of wine. The bed and breakfast is just as charming, being a historic colonial homestead hidden from the street by a large lawn and leafy trees. My favorite wine at Jessie Creek was their Merlot, which was dry and medium-bodied, finished with a bit of spice, and would be perfect with a BBQ steak.

Address: 1 N. Delsea Drive (Route 47), Cape May Court House, NJ

Phone: (609) 536-2092

Website: www.jessiecreekwinery.com

E-mail: artreale@yahoo.com

Appellation: Outer Coastal Plain

First vines planted: 2002

Opened to the public: 2012

Key people: Juan Fernandez, Bruce Morrison, Art Reale (owners)

Acres cultivated: 5

Cases/year: 1,200

Grapes: Cabernet Sauvignon, Chambourcin, Chardonnay, Concord, Merlot and Pinot Gris

Other fruit: cranberries

Other attractions: bed and breakfast, weddings

Days: daily tastings

Hawk Haven Vineyard & Winery

The Wuerker family has farmed in Rio Grande since 1940. Originally they were lima bean and dairy farmers, but in 1997 they planted Cabernet Sauvignon grapes. Twelve years later Todd and Kenna Wuerker opened Hawk Haven. The vineyard's name refers to the large number of hawks that migrate to the farm every year, and many of their wines are also hawk themed (e.g, Talon). Grape cultivation is overseen by viticulturalist Lalo Serra.

The tasting room is located in an imposing concrete and stone building with a distinctive arched entrance. The winery has been chosen to be a test site for a Rutgers University study, and last year, they planted Lagrein and Teroldego grapes, two very rare red grapes from Trentino-South Tyrol region of Italy. Researchers are studying whether grapes from this region of Italy can be successfully grown in New Jersey. My favorite was Red-Tailed Rose, a blend of White Cabernet Sauvignon, White Zinfindel, and Vidal Blanc, which was sweet with a smooth finish.

Address: 600 South Railroad Avenue, Rio Grande, NJ

Phone: (609) 846-7347

Website: hawkhavenvin.wordpress.com

E-mail: info@hawkhavenvineyard.com

Appellation: Outer Coastal Plain

First vines planted: 1997

Opened to the public: 2009

Key people: Todd & Kenna Wuerker (owners); Lalo Serra (viticulturalist)

Acres cultivated: 9

Cases/year: 4,200

Grapes: Albariño, Cabernet Franc, Cabernet Sauvignon, Chambourcin, Chardonnay, Gewürztraminer, Lagrein, Merlot, Petit Verdot, Pinot Gris, Riesling, Sangiovese, Sauvignon Blanc, Syrah, Teroldego, Tempranillo, Vidal Blanc, Viognier, and Zinfandel

Other fruit: N/A

Other attractions: pet-friendly, picnicking

Days: tastings daily, tours on weekends

Cape May Winery & Vineyard

The first New Jersey wine that I ever tasted was from Cape May Winery, which at the time was very small and did not have a tasting room. In 1992, Bill and Joan Hayes planted a vineyard in North Cape May, and three years later started selling wine. In 2002, the Hayes family sold the winery to Arthur "Toby" Craig, who hired professional winemaker Darren Hesington. Today, Cape May Winery is among the most visited vineyards in the state.

Reflecting the winery's coastal location, the parking lot consists of broken-up seashells. The tasting facility has an outdoor deck with a spectacular view of their grape vines. They have a separate brand, Issac Smith, named after a coffin maker from the 1820s who owned the land where one of the vineyards now lies. I strongly recommend Fini Blanc, a dessert wine that has 8% residual sugar. Not surprisingly, this wine is very sweet and fruity. I could see myself sipping this while eating a large piece of chocolate cake.

Address: 711 Townbank Road, North Cape May, NJ

Phone: (609) 884-1169

Website: www.capemaywinery.com

E-mail: manager@capemaywinery.com

Appellation: Outer Coastal Plain

Other labels: Isaac Smith

First vines planted: 1992

Opened to the public: 1995

Key people: Bill & Joan Hayes (founders); Toby Craig (owner); Darren Hesington (winemaker)

Acres cultivated: 25

Cases/year: 11,000

Grapes: Albariño, Cabernet Franc, Cabernet Sauvignon, Cayuga White, Chambourcin, Chardonnay, Colombard, Merlot, Pinot Gris, Pinot Noir, Riesling, Sauvignon Blanc, Syrah, Vidal Blanc, Viognier, and Zinfandel

Other fruit: apples

Other attractions: pet-friendly, picnicking

Days: daily tastings and tours

Turdo Vineyards & Winery

Salvatore Turdo (pronounced *tour-doe*) is an electrical contractor from Northern New Jersey. He immigrated to the United States from Sicily at age 14. As part of their future retirement plans, Sal and his wife Sara bought a woodlot in North Cape May, believing that the area's maritime climate and sandy soils would be good for growing grapes. In 1999, they cleared the land and planted grapes, and five years later Turdo Vineyards opened to the public.

In 2010, their son Luca expanded the family business by making his own wines using grapes grown at a nearby farm in Cape May County, and these vintages are labeled DiLuca. All of Turdo's wines are made with minimal sulfites, and the entire facility is powered exclusively with solar energy. They are the only winery east of the Mississippi to use Nero d'Avola, an intensely aromatic grape that is indigenous to Sicily. I very much liked their signature Nero d'Avola wine, which started soft and fruity, but ended with a burst of tannins.

Address: 3911 Bayshore Road, North Cape May, NJ

Phone: (609) 884-5591

Website: www.turdovineyards.com

E-mail: luca@turdovineyards.com

Appellation: Outer Coastal Plain

Other labels: DiLuca

First vines planted: 1999

Opened to the public: 2004

Key people: Sal & Sara Turdo, Luca Turdo (owners)

Acres cultivated: 5

Cases/year: 1,100

Grapes: Albariño, Barbera, Cabernet Sauvignon, Merlot, Nebbiolo, Nero d'Avola, Pinot Gris, Pinot Noir, Riesling, Sangiovese, Sauvignon Blanc, and Syrah

Other fruit: N/A

Signature wine: Nero d'Avola

Other attractions: pet-friendly, solar-powered, weddings

Days: daily tastings in summer, Fri. and Sat. in May and Sept., closed remainder of year

Willow Creek Winery

Barbara Bray Wilde purchased a former produce farm in 1998, and in 2005 she began to cultivate wine grapes. Wilde became interested in wine as a student at the University of California at Berkeley, and she has stated that the climate of the Cape May area is similar to the wine valleys of Northern California. The farm, named for a large willow tree and meandering creek on the property, has chickens, turkeys, honeybees, and a wide array of crops. The vineyard is tended by viticulturalist Kevin Celli who formerly oversaw grape growing at Natali Vineyards.

The tasting facility, which opened in 2012, is a large building that was built by Amish workers from Pennsylvania. Willow Creek is the sole producer in New Jersey of Malvasia Bianca, a white *vinifera* grape indigenous to the northwest coast of Italy. Their non-estate wines are labeled Wilde Cock, a reference to the owner and her beloved roosters. I recommend the Bacchus Red, a Bordeaux-like blend of Merlot, Chambourcin and Cabernet Sauvignon that pairs nicely with a steak.

Address: 160-168 Stevens Street, West Cape May, NJ

Phone: (609) 770-8782

Website: willowcreekwinerycapemay.com

E-mail: willowcreekwinery@gmail.com

Appellation: Outer Coastal Plain

Other labels: Wilde Cock

First vines planted: 2005

Opened to the public: 2012

Key people: Barbara Bray Wilde (owner), Kevin Celli (viticulturalist)

Acres cultivated: 40

Cases/year: 6,000

Grapes: Albariño, Cabernet Franc, Cabernet Sauvignon, Chambourcin, Corot Noir, Malbec, Malvasia Bianca, Merlot, Muscat Blanc, Pinot Noir, Riesling, Sangiovese, Sauvignon Blanc, Seyval Blanc, and Syrah

Other fruit: apples, pumpkins

Other attractions: picnicking, weddings

Other products: eggs, flowers, fruits, honey, poultry, tobacco, vegetables, wormwood

Open: daily tours and tastings

Introduction to the Farm Belt

Burlington, Camden, Cumberland, Gloucester and Salem counties are the reason New Jersey is called the Garden State. The Farm Belt region is unknown to many residents of the state, being sparsely populated and far from the state's urban centers. The southwestern corner of New Jersey is the state's breadbasket, being blessed with great soil and a mild climate. Here agriculture is often a full-time occupation with families owning farms for generations.

Drive through this region, and you will see an abundance of fruit and vegetable farms, interspersed by dense woods and undisturbed marshland. Every so often, you'll encounter a village that looks like it hasn't changed much in the last century. Because of the Farm Belt's strong religious heritage, many of the towns are dry. Nevertheless, because of the profitability of wine grapes and the fact that winery licenses are issued by the state irrespective of municipal liquor laws, the number of wineries in the Farm Belt has exploded in recent years.

Most of these wineries are part of the Outer Coastal Plain Viticultural Area. Many are farms that converted part or all of their land from other crops to potentially more lucrative wine grapes. Like the Southern Shore, it is very possible to grow French, Italian, and Spanish grapes in the Farm Belt. However, because this area has far less tourists than the shore, the tasting rooms are often staffed by the owners, and with a few exceptions their prices are lower. Reflecting the unhurried pace of life in this region, I spent much more time visiting these wineries, enjoying good conversations while tasting fine vintages.

The sixteen vineyards in this section are connected by a jumble of often poorly-marked country roads, and I made several wrong turns on my first visit. The book has three wine trails for the Farm Belt region. The first five wineries are in an area heavily dominated by pinelands. The second road trip traverses miles of farm land and marsh near the Delaware River. The last trail starts near the sleepy towns of Mullica Hill and Glassboro, and later involves driving though some of the most remote parts of New Jersey.

Road Trip #6

Wineries:

1. DeMastro Vineyards & Winery
2. Valenzano Winery
3. Amalthea Cellars
4. Sharrott Winery
5. Coda Rossa Winery

Restaurants/Eateries:

Vincentown Diner – Conveniently located on Route 206, much of the food at this diner comes from local farms, including fresh produce, organic eggs, free range beef, and wines from Valenzano and DeMastro. I recommend their homemade soups and delicious burgers.
Address: 2357 Vincentown Columbus Rd (Route 206), Vincentown, NJ
Phone: (609) 267-3033

British Chip Shop – Situated in the heart of historic Haddonfield, this restaurant celebrates the cuisine of the British Isles. Offering lunch, dinner, and Sunday brunch, the British Chip Shop serves both traditional favorites like Welsh rarebit and modern dishes like curried cheese chips.
Address: 146 Kings Highway East, Haddonfield, NJ
Phone: (856) 354-0204

Brother Bear's BBQ – Brother Bear's has mastered barbecuing, slowly cooking top-quality meat with homemade sauces using a wood fire. Stop by this combination food truck and roadside stand, and order their amazingly tender ribs and mouth-watering pulled pork sandwiches.
Address: 53 White Horse Pike (Route 30), Chesilhurst, NJ
Phone: (856) 628-1888

Lodging:

Isaac Hilliard House – Build in the Federal style of the mid-1800s, this beautiful inn is located in the small community of Pemberton in the heart of the New Jersey Pine Barrens. Besides all the normal amenities of a B&B, the Issac Hillard House also has an in-ground swimming pool.
Address: 31 Hanover Street, Pemberton, NJ
Phone: (609) 894-0756

Haddonfield Inn – This bed and breakfast combines Victorian-era charm with international flair. Situated in the historic district of Haddonfield, the eight guest rooms and one suite at this inn are each uniquely decorated with themes like Japanese sleekness or African safari.
Address: 44 West End Ave, Haddonfield, NJ
Phone: (856) 428-2195

Attractions:

Columbus Farmers' Market – Everything from farm-fresh produce to fine art to tractor parts can be purchased at the Columbus Market. Located on Route 206, this gigantic bazaar has 65 indoor stores, and one of the only remaining flea markets in New Jersey.
Address: 2919 Route 206, Columbus, NJ
Phone: (609) 267-0400

Indian King Tavern – Haddonfield has been a dry town since 1873, but nearly a hundred years earlier, the New Jersey colonial assembly met here and declared New Jersey to be independent from Great Britain. The tavern was the state's first recognized historic site, and today is a museum depicting colonial life in New Jersey.
Address: 233 Kings Highway East, Haddonfield, NJ
Phone: (856) 429-6792

DeMastro Vineyards & Winery

DeMastro Vineyards is a hidden gem. It's one the smallest wineries in the state, producing only 300 cases per year, is not a member of any winegrowing associations, and doesn't take part in any wine festivals. However, DeMastro offers top-quality wines and unforgettable hospitality. The winery is named for its owners, Mary DeSantis and Angelo Mastropieri, who first planted grapes on their Vincentown property in 1991. Initially the couple only made wine for their family and friends, but in 2009 they opened to the public.

The winery is located on a secluded road in the Pine Barrens, and has a small cellar-like tasting room. Angelo formerly grew grapes with his father in Italy, and their winery is very European in character, exclusively using *vinifera* grapes, and having a limited variety of vintages. I strongly recommend all of their wines, but the best one was their Chardonnay. Moderately dry and lightly oaked, this full-bodied white wine would go perfectly with salmon.

Address: 436 Ongs Hat Road, Southampton, NJ

Phone: (609) 859-0916

Website: www.demastrovineyards.us

E-mail: amastropieri@netzero.com

Appellation: Outer Coastal Plain

First vines planted: 1991

Opened to the public: 2009

Key people: Mary DeSantis, Angelo Mastropieri

Acres: 4

Cases/year: 300

Grapes: Cabernet Sauvignon, Chardonnay, Merlot, and Pinot Noir

Other fruit: N/A

Days: tastings on Saturday and by appointment on Sunday

Valenzano Winery

Valenzano Winery has become one of the largest and best known wineries in New Jersey. In 1974, Anthony "Tony" Valenzano Sr. started a farm in Shamong, which is deep in the New Jersey Pine Barrens. He raised livestock and grew grains, and as a hobby made wine. In 1991, Tony and his sons Mark and Anthony Jr. planted a vineyard, and five years later the winery made its debut. Valenzano is powered by solar energy and is heated with steam that comes from 60 feet below the earth.

The tasting facility looks like a wedding hall, and a lot of weddings are held here. Every September since 2002, Valenzano has hosted "WineFest," an event that typically over 10,000 people attend. They are the only Garden State winery to produce mead. Valenzano prides itself on their affordable prices – there are no tasting fees and most of their wines are in the $10-12 range. Try their Sweet Cab, which smells dry and initially tastes dry, but finishes sweet. Pair this enigmatic wine with a chocolate cannoli.

Address: 1090 Route 206, Shamong, NJ

Phone: (609) 268-6731

Website: valenzanowine.com

E-mail: tony@valenzanowine.com

Appellation: Outer Coastal Plain

First vines planted: 1991

Opened to the public: 1996

Key people: Anthony Valenzano Sr., Anthony Valenzano Jr., Mark Valenzano (owners)

Acres cultivated: 44

Cases/year: 40,000

Grapes: Cabernet Franc, Cabernet Sauvignon, Chambourcin, Chardonnay, Concord, Fredonia, Ives Noir, Merlot, Niagara, Norton (Cynthiana), Vidal Blanc, and Zinfandel

Other fruit: apples, blueberries, cranberries, honey (for mead), peaches, plums, raspberries, and pumpkins

Other attractions: pet-friendly, picnicking, solar-powered, and weddings

Days: daily tastings, tours by appointment

Amalthea Cellars

Winemaker Louis Caracciolo of Amalthea Cellars considers himself both an artist and a scientist. In 1976 he planted grapes in the town of Atco, and five years later the winery, which is named after a moon of Jupiter, opened to the public. Amalthea (pronounced *am-ul-thee-a*) uses traditional winemaking techniques. Caracciolo advocates a philosophy that he calls "The Third Wave" or "The Archaic Revival" where the vintner takes a hands-off approach, and lets the wine develop without any chemical or mechanical intervention.

The winery is in a nineteenth-century chalet-style farmhouse. There is a door for the Green Dragon Tavern which was named after the famous watering hole in Boston. The Green Dragon Tavern was formerly a restaurant but now is only used for special events. It is the only winery in the state to use Rayon d'Or, which is a white hybrid grape developed in France in the early twentieth century. Try their Chardonnay Reserve, a full-bodied white aged in French Oak for a year. I could see myself drinking this wine while eating salmon.

Address: 209 Vineyard Road, Atco, NJ

Phone: (856) 768-8585

Website: amaltheacellars.com

E-mail: winery@amaltheacellars.com

Appellation: Outer Coastal Plain

First vines planted: 1976

Opened to the public: 1981

Key people: Louis Caracciolo (owner)

Acres cultivated: 10

Cases/year: 5,000

Grapes: Cabernet Franc, Cabernet Sauvignon, Chancellor, Chardonnay, Dolcetto, Merlot, Pinot Gris, Rayon d'Or, Riesling, Rkatsiteli, Sauvignon Blanc, Syrah, Traminette, Villard Blanc, and Viognier

Other fruit: blueberries and peaches

Other attractions: picnicking, weddings

Days: tastings on Friday, Saturday, and Sunday

Sharrott Winery

Sharrott Winery takes a scientific approach to winemaking. A little over a decade ago, Larry Sharrott Jr. and his son Larry III attended seminars sponsored by Rutgers University, and then enrolled in viticulture and winemaking classes offered through the University of California at Davis. In 2005, they planted grapes in a former apple orchard in Blue Anchor, a small town in the New Jersey Pine Barrens. Three years later, the tasting room opened.

Being environmentally conscious, the entire facility is solar-powered, and manure is the primary fertilizer. Sharrott (pronounced *shar-it*) frequently holds events at the vineyard, and enters their vintages into a number of major wine competitions each year. At the 2009 Finger Lakes competition, which included more than 500 wineries from 22 countries, Sharrott won Best Chardonnay. They have the best Chambourcin that I've ever tasted. Dry, strong, and smooth, this very masculine wine needs to be accompanied by a giant steak or game meat.

Address: 370 South Egg Harbor Road, Blue Anchor, NJ

Phone: (609) 567-9463

Website: sharrottwinery.com

E-mail: contact@sharrottwinery.com

Appellation: Outer Coastal Plain

First vines planted: 2005

Opened to the public: 2008

Key people: Larry Sharrott Jr, Larry Sharrott III (owners)

Acres cultivated: 6

Cases/year: 4,000

Grapes: Cabernet Franc, Cabernet Sauvignon, Chambourcin, Chardonnay, Fredonia, Merlot, Pinot Gris, Riesling, Vidal Blanc, and Vignoles (Ravat 51)

Other fruit: blueberries, cranberries, and peaches

Days: daily tastings, tours on weekends

Coda Rossa Winery

Kenton and Kathy Nice wound up owning a winery because of what they describe as a "hobby entirely out of control." The South Jersey couple first made wine for their own consumption, and then in 2004 opened the Wine Room of Cherry Hill, an instructional winemaking facility. Two years later the Nices purchased an abandoned vineyard in Franklinville. They refurbished the property, and the winery opened to the public in 2010.

Coda Rossa's vineyard is highly attractive, with meticulously maintained grapes and roses growing at the end of each row. Red-tailed hawks fly around the farm, and the winery's name is an Italian translation of "red-tailed." The vast majority of Coda Rossa's vintages are dry reds, with a handful of whites and sweet wines. Blue Moon Port is their most unique vintage, being made from Merlot blended with blueberries. It was strong-bodied with a velvety texture, and rather than imparting tartness, the blueberries balance the sweetness of the port.

Address: 1526 Dutch Mill Road, Franklinville, NJ

Phone: (856) 697-9463

Website: www.codarossa.com

E-mail: info@codarossa.com

Appellation: Outer Coastal Plain

First vines planted: 2002

Opened to the public: 2010

Key people: Kenton and Kathy Nice (owners)

Acres: 10

Cases/year: 1,500

Grapes: Barbera, Cabernet Franc, Cabernet Sauvignon, Cayuga White, Chambourcin, Chardonnay, Concord, Durif (Petite Sirah), Merlot, Nebbiolo, Niagara, Pinot Gris, Sangiovese, Sauvignon Blanc, Syrah, Vidal Blanc, and Zinfandel

Other fruit: blackberries, blueberries, peaches and raspberries

Other attractions: instructional winemaking

Days: tastings on Friday, Saturday and Sunday

Road Trip #7

Wineries:

1. DiBella Winery
2. Cedarvale Winery
3. Salem Oak Vineyards
4. Auburn Road Vineyards
5. Chestnut Run Farm

Restaurants/Eateries:

Rode's Fireside Restaurant & Tavern – For over 120 years, the Rode family has sold food to residents of Gloucester County, as poultry farmers, at a BBQ chicken takeout, and today at a home-style restaurant. Cozy up by one of their fireplaces, and enjoy a barbeque chicken dinner.
Address: 533 Kings Highway, Woolwich, NJ
Phone: (856) 467-2700

Ye Olde Centerton Inn – This is the oldest inn in New Jersey, and the second oldest in the United States, and Revolutionary heroes such as Marquis de Lafayette and Mad Anthony Wayne stopped here. Today this landmark restaurant is known for its seafood dishes.
Address: 1136 Almond Road, Elmer, NJ
Phone: (856) 358-3201

Ginger Cake Café – Nothing is better on a cold day than a hot cup of tea and baked goodies. Named for the owner's homemade ginger cakes, this café in downtown Woodstown offers over 50 different types of tea, and an assortment of delicious sandwiches, soups, and desserts.
Address: 10 South Main Street, Woodstown, NJ
Phone: (856) 769-0141

Lodging:

Barrett's Plantation House – The original portions of this historic bed and breakfast date to 1735. Bald eagles are commonly seen at this brick farmhouse located near the 6000-acre Mannington Meadow. Many guests of Barrett's Plantation report that ghosts occupy the inn.
Address: 203 Old Kings Highway, Mannington, NJ
Phone: (856) 935-0812

Four Seasons Family Campground – Cabins and trailers can be rented at this wooded campground in Pilesgrove. Four Seasons has a pond for swimming and fishing, an activities director for children, and a variety of sporting and recreational facilities.
Address: 158 Woodstown Daretown Road, Pilesgrove, NJ
Phone: (856) 769-3635

Attractions:

Bridgeport Speedway – Since 1972, stock cars have been racing here. Bridgeport's 5/8" of a mile oval is considered the fastest dirt track in the eastern United States. Races are held on weekends from spring to fall, and camping spaces can be reserved.
Address: 83 Floodgates Road, Swedesboro, NJ
Phone: (856) 467-4407

Cowtown Rodeo – If you don't think that rodeos and New Jersey go together, you haven't been to Cowtown which has the oldest weekly rodeo in the United States. Since 1929, Garden State cowboys have come here to ride broncos and bulls, and lasso steers and calves.
Address: 780 Harding Highway (Route 40), Pilesgrove, NJ
Phone: (856) 769-3200

DiBella Winery

The DiBellas are fourth-generation farmers, having farmed in Woolwich since 1925. Over time, the family has raised cattle, grains, fruits, and vegetables. Twenty-five years ago, they became the first farmers in Gloucester County to take part in the state's farmland preservation program. Will and Julie DiBella planted grapes in 2002 to augment their 150 acres of wheat and soybeans. Eight years later, they began selling wine.

Will oversees the cultivation of the grapes, and Julie runs the tasting room. Under state preservation laws, no new permanent structures can be built on their land, and so tasting takes place in a very cute tent adjacent to their farmhouse. Julie is very personable, and their wines are as unpretentious as their farm. My favorite wine was their Lampone Delicato Raspberry Merlot, which combines the velvety tannic flavor of a Merlot with the intense sweetness of raspberries. Sip this unique wine while savoring chocolate truffles.

Address: 229 Davidson Road, Woolwich, NJ

Phone: (609) 221-6201

Website: www.dibellawinery.com

E-mail: dibellawinery@yahoo.com

Appellation: Outer Coastal Plain

First vines planted: 2002

Opened to the public: 2010

Key people: Will & Julie DiBella (owners)

Acres: 4

Cases/year: 900

Grapes: Cabernet Franc, Cabernet Sauvignon, Chardonnay, Merlot, Pinot Gris and Traminette

Other fruit: cherries and raspberries

Days: tastings on weekends

Cedarvale Winery

Cedarvale Winery is a truly enjoyable place to visit. Upon entering the tasting room, I was greeted by the bubbly and vivacious Marsha Gaventa. Since 1905, the Gaventa family has owned a produce farm in the cedar swamps of Logan Township for which the winery is named. The farm was honored by the Gloucester County Board of Agriculture for utilizing innovative techniques to reduce the usage of pesticides and water. In 2004, Marsha and her husband Ed added grapevines to their array of crops, and four years later their tasting room opened.

Cedarvale's tasting room is cozy and replete with wine paraphernalia. The Gaventas make wine from apples, cherries, nectarines, and other fruits grown on the farm. Though they only make a handful of grape vintages, they are of top quality. In 2013, their Cabernet Franc won the Governor's Cup for best grape wine in the state. Reflecting Cedarvale's effervescent charm, this award-winning wine bursts with burgundy color and peppery tannins.

Address: 205 Repaupo Station Road, Logan, NJ

Phone: (856) 467-3088

Website: www.cedarvalewinery.com

E-mail: info@cedarvalewinery.com

Appellation: N/A

First vines planted: 2004

Opened to the public: 2008

Key people: Ed & Marsha Gaventa

Acres cultivated: 8

Cases/year: 2,500

Grapes: Cabernet Franc, Merlot, Pinot Gris, and Villard Blanc

Other fruit: apples, blueberries, cherries, nectarines, and strawberries

Other attractions: picnicking

Days: tastings Thursday to Sunday

Salem Oak Vineyards

If you don't think that French winemaking goes with small town America, you haven't visited Salem Oak Vineyards. Mandi Cassidy's comes from a family of winemakers in France, and in 2003 she planted a vineyard in the village of Pedricktown. The winery, which is named for a legendary oak tree where English settlers made a peace treaty with Native Americans, opened a decade later. Unlike most wineries that are located along country roads, Salem Oak is right in the heart of Pedricktown, an otherwise dry community.

The inside of the winery is spacious and has large murals of historic events. My visit to Salem Oak was very enjoyable – their very friendly dog greeted me at the door, and my server was a great storyteller. Most of their wines are named for members of Mandi's family, and they are the only winery in the state to use Rougeon, a hybrid grape known for its intense red color. Their most fun wine was Triple Twin, a blush-colored strawberry wine which is served with chocolate shavings.

Address: 60 North Railroad Avenue, Pedricktown, NJ

Phone: (856) 889-2121

Website: www.salemoakvineyards.com

E-mail: salemoakvineyards@gmail.com

Appellation: N/A

First vines planted: 2003

Opened to the public: 2013

Key people: Mandi Cassidy (owner)

Acres cultivated: 4

Cases/year: 900

Grapes: Chardonnay, Cabernet Franc, Cabernet Sauvignon, Cayuga White, Concord, Niagara, Petite Sirah, Pinot Gris, Pinot Noir, Rougeon, Seyval Blanc, and Vidal Blanc

Other fruit: strawberries

Other attractions: pet-friendly, picnicking, weddings

Days: tastings Thursday to Sunday

Auburn Road Vineyards

    Most New Jersey wineries were founded by people with a winemaking or agricultural background. On the other hand, Auburn Road came about as result of six friends with a lot of ambition. In 2004, these former lawyers and financial advisors planted a vineyard, and three years later the winery opened to the public. Despite their limited experience, Auburn Road is one of the most popular wineries in the state, and when I visited the place was packed.

    The winery, named after the street where two of the owners reside, is located on a picturesque country road in Pilesgrove. Their tasting room, which they refer to as the Enoteca, is in a large wood shingle building. Besides being a wine bar, the Enoteca is a bistro that serves soups, cheeses, and breads, and offers a five-course dinner on Friday nights. I recommend Rustica, a blend of Cabernet Franc, Cabernet Sauvignon, and Chambourcin which tastes like a spicy Bordeaux, and would pair very well with spare ribs.

Address: 117 Sharptown Auburn Road, Pilesgrove, NJ

Phone: (856) 769-9463

Website: www.auburnroadvineyards.com

E-mail: info@auburnroadvineyards.com

Appellation: Outer Coastal Plain

First vines planted: 2004

Opened to the public: 2007

Key people: Dave Davis, Julienne Donnini, Scott Donnini, Jennifer Kilpatrick, Shannon Kilpatrick, Joe Reilly (owners)

Acres cultivated: 19

Cases/year: 4,200

Grapes: Cabernet Franc, Cabernet Sauvignon, Cayuga White, Chambourcin, Chardonnay, Merlot, Niagara, Pinot Gris, Sangiovese, and Vidal Blanc

Other fruit: apples, blueberries and peaches

Other attractions: bistro, weddings

Days: tastings Thursday to Monday, tours Friday to Sunday

Chestnut Run Farm

Chestnut Run Farm advertises that "absolutely no grapes are harmed in the making of these wines."   Instead all of their wines are made from Asian pears, Fuji apples, and Shiro plums. Bob and Lise Clark bought a farm in Pilesgrove in 1986, and planted a variety of crops including fruit trees. Because of declining produce prices, the Clarks needed to find a way to save the farm, which is named after a stream bordering the property. Like many other growers, they discovered that the liquid form of their fruit was far more lucrative, and in 2007 they began to sell wine.

Due to restrictions on preserved farmland, Chestnut Run Farm did not sell on-site for several years, distributing their wines only at festivals and through local liquor stores. Since 2012, they've had a cute roadside tasting room which is open by appointment. Of their five wines, my favorite is their Spiced Sweet Asian Pear wine, which is Chestnut Run's sweetest and is flavored with ginger. Treat yourself to Peking duck and a glass of this special vintage.

Address: 66 Stewart Road Pilesgrove, NJ

Phone: (856) 769-2158

Website: www.chestnutrunfarm.com

E-mail: chestnutrunfarm@aol.com

Appellation: Outer Coastal Plain

First planted: 1986 (fruit trees)

Opened to the public: 2007

Key people: Bob & Lise Clark (owners)

Acres cultivated: 5

Cases/year: 700

Grapes: N/A

Other fruit: Asian pears, Fuji apples, Shiro plums

Days: tastings by appointment

Road Trip #8

Wineries:

1. Wagonhouse Winery
2. Heritage Vineyards
3. Summit City Farms & Winery
4. Monroeville Vineyard & Winery
5. Southwind Vineyard & Winery

Restaurants/Eateries:

Lake House Restaurant – This impressive structure overlooking Lake Iona has served as an inn, dance hall, speakeasy, and brothel, and is now a popular restaurant. Get a seat overlooking the lake, buy a sandwich and a drink, and don't let the resident ghosts scare you away.
Address: 611 Taylor Road, Newfield, NJ
Phone: (856) 694-5700

Aunt Betty's Kitchen – Sometimes while travelling you just want to stop somewhere for comfort food. This small but charming café in the historic village of Greenwich has a regular menu and blackboard specials. The owner is known as Aunt Betty, and people come far for her omelets, soups, and desserts.
Address: 1016 Ye Greate Street, Greenwich, NJ
Phone: (856) 451-2400

Bayshore Crab House – Cumberland County has a long history of fishing and boatbuilding. Enjoy the fruits of the bay at this seafood shack located in a barn on the banks of the Nantuxent Creek. Enjoy the maritime memorabilia, and order yourself a plate of New Jersey oysters.
Address: 100 Back Road, Cedarville, NJ
Phone: (856) 447-4535

Lodging:

Candle House Inn – This contemporary house is located on 34 acres in South Harrison, where the owners raise horses and chickens. Guests can walk the trails through the pastures and woods and observe deer, turkeys, and eagles, or simply unwind by the in-ground pool.
Address: 639 Tomlin Station Road (Route 607), South Harrison, NJ
Phone: (856) 981-9443

Charlesworth Hotel & Restaurant – There are very few places in New Jersey where you can watch the sunset over the water. Though damaged by Hurricane Sandy and still closed as of the writing of this book, this iconic B&B and seafood restaurant plans to reopen in 2015.
Address: 224 New Jersey Avenue, Fortescue, NJ
Phone: (856) 447-4928

Attractions:

A.J. Meerwald – This is the official tall ship of New Jersey. Launched in 1928 as an oyster dredging schooner, today the 115-foot *Meerwald* is on the National Register of Historic Places. Visit the adjacent Delaware Bay Museum, and then take a sail on this beautiful boat.
Address: 2800 High Street, Port Norris , NJ
Phone: (800) 485-3072

Delsea Drive-In Theatre – New Jersey was the birthplace of the drive-in theatre, but by 1991 all of them had closed. However, the Delsea Drive-In reopened in 2004, and today the sound is broadcast through your car radio. Buy your bag of popcorn, and let the show begin.
Address: 2203 South Delsea Drive (Route 47), Vineland, NJ
Phone: (856) 696-0011

Wagonhouse Winery

Since the nineteenth century, the Browns have been farming in Gloucester County, growing fruits and vegetables, and raising cows, hogs, and poultry. In 2004, Dan and Heather Brown leased land in Mickleton from his family and planted grapes. A year later they opened a winery which is named after a wagon house on the property. In 2011, Wagonhouse moved to a larger facility in South Harrison. The tasting room is quite attractive, with hardwood floors and an old-fashioned shuffleboard table.

When I visited, the tasting consisted of nearly twenty different wines. Their dry wines are sold under the Wagonhouse name, whereas their sweet wines are labeled as Three Boys Brand, a reference to Dan and Heather's three sons. Wagonhouse is the only producer in New Jersey of Pinotage, which is a red *vinifera* grape developed in South Africa in 1925. My favorite was their Chardonnay, a dry yet citrusy wine that would go perfectly with scallops.

Address: 1401 Woodstown Mullica Hill Rd (Route 45), Swedesboro, NJ

Phone: (609) 780-8019

Website: www.wagonhousewinery.com

E-mail: info@wagonhousewinery.com

Appellation: Outer Coastal Plain

Other labels: Three Boys Brand

First vines planted: 2004

Opened to the public: 2005

Moved to new location: 2011

Key people: Dan & Heather Brown (owners)

Acres cultivated: 10

Cases/year: 7,000

Grapes: Barbera, Cabernet Franc, Cabernet Sauvignon, Chardonnay, Merlot, Pinotage, Pinot Gris, Sangiovese, Sauvignon Blanc, Syrah, Vidal Blanc, and Viognier

Other fruit: almonds, blueberries, cranberries, mangoes, peaches, pomegranates and strawberries

Other attractions: picnicking

Days: tastings Thursday to Monday

Heritage Vineyards

The Heritage family has been farming in Mullica Hill since 1853. However by the 1990s, they thought that might have to sell their farm because it had become unprofitable to grow peaches. Though they had no experience with winemaking, Bill and Penni Heritage took a chance and in 1998 planted grapes. Four years later they sold their first bottle of wine. The first time I visited Heritage, they had a farm stand with a small counter for tasting, and few people had heard of them. Today, that farm stand is a tasting room, and their vintages routinely win top awards.

The inside of the winery is spacious and wide-open with a wooden bar in the center. Heritage's vintner, Sean Comninos, developed their signature BDX, a Bordeaux-style wine which scored near the top at the Judgment of Princeton. Reflecting the farm's history, Heritage also makes wine from a variety of other fruits. My favorite wine was their sugar plum, which no other winery in the state produces. This uncommon wine oozed with candy-like sweetness, and pairs well with homemade ice cream.

Address: 480 Mullica Hill Road (Route 322), Mullica Hill, NJ

Phone: (856) 589-4474

Website: www.heritagewinenj.com

E-mail: rich@heritagewinenj.com

Appellation: Outer Coastal Plain

First vines planted: 1998

Opened to the public: 2002

Key people: Bill & Penni Heritage, Richard Heritage (owners); Sean Comninos (winemaker)

Acres cultivated: 40

Cases/year: 13,000

Grapes: Cabernet Franc, Cabernet Sauvignon, Chambourcin, Chardonnay, Concord, Grenache, Malbec, Merlot, Muscat Blanc, Petit Verdot, Pinot Gris, Pinot Noir, Sauvignon Blanc, Sémillon, and Syrah

Other fruit: apples, blueberries, peaches, and sugar plums

Signature wine: BDX

Other attractions: fruit picking, pet friendly, petting zoo, and picnicking

Days: daily tastings, tours on Saturday

Summit City Farms & Winery

Summit City Winery is named for a landmark conference between Lyndon Johnson and Soviet Premier Alexei Kosygin that occurred in 1967 in Glassboro. Since 1922, the DeEugenio family have been farming in the Glassboro area. Lewis DeEugenio Sr., his son Lewis DeEugenio Jr., and his daughter-in-law Leila DeEugenio cultivate more than 500 acres of apples, nectarines, peaches, nectarines, and other fruits and vegetables. Last year they added grapes to their assortment of crops, and their tasting room opened in the summer 2014.

The winery looks like a fruit market from the outside, but the inside has attractive wood-paneled walls and historic memorabilia. Besides fruits and wine, the farm also offers pony rides during the summer. While Summit City has traditional dry wines, they also offer more than ten different types of fruit wine. My favorite was their Jersey Queen Peach, which had the sweetness of fresh-squeezed juice but the smooth finish of a sophisticated white wine.

Address: 500 University Boulevard, Glassboro, NJ

Phone: 856-881-2930

Website: www.summitcityfarms.com

E-mail: leilade@comcast.net

Appellation: Outer Coastal Plain

First vines planted: 2013

Opened to the public: 2014

Key people: Lewis DeEugenio Sr., Lewis DeEugenio Jr., Leila DeEugenio (owners)

Acres cultivated: 15

Cases/year: 700

Grapes: Cabernet Sauvignon, Chardonnay, Concord, Niagara, Pinot Grigio, Syrah, and Traminette

Other fruit: apples, blueberries, cherries, mangoes, nectarines, peaches, and pumpkins

Other attractions: pony rides

Other products: fruit and vegetables

Days: tastings Friday to Sunday

Monroeville Vineyard & Winery

John Basile is a fourth-generation home winemaker. In 2009, he and his wife Debra decided to go a step further, and purchased a farm in the sleepy community of Monroeville in Salem County. The following year they planted grapes, and in 2012 their tasting room opened. Despite coming from a home vintner background, the couple utilizes scientific winemaking and innovative agricultural methods. Kevin Martin serves as Monroeville's viticulturalist.

The tasting room is located in a traditional red barn, and has bar-style tables and stools for patrons. Although it was crowded when I visited, John and Debra were quite friendly. Like many of the vineyards of the Outer Coastal Plain, they have a number of fruit wines. However, Monroeville also has varietals such as Grüner Veltliner and Muscat of Alexandria which are very uncommon in southern New Jersey. The Grüner Veltliner was sharp and dry, and would pair quite well with a plate of cheddar cheese.

Address: 314 Richwood Road, Monroeville, NJ

Phone: (856) 521-0523

Website: monroevillewinery.net

E-mail: debrabasile@monroevillewinery.comcastbiz.net

Appellation: Outer Coastal Plain

First vines planted: 2010

Opened to the public: 2012

Key people: John & Debra Basile (owners); Kevin Martin (viticulturalist)

Acres cultivated: 4

Cases/year: 1,800

Grapes: Cabernet Franc, Cabernet Sauvignon, Chardonnay, Concord, Grüner Veltliner, Merlot, Muscat of Alexandria, Pinot Gris, and Syrah

Other fruit: apples, blueberries, cranberries, nectarines, peaches, and strawberries

Days: tastings Thursday to Sunday

Southwind Vineyard & Winery

Since 1978, the Allen family has owned a horse farm in Deerfield. Lorre Allen and her husband Joseph Riley bought the homestead from her parents and in 2006 planted grapes. Six years later, they began selling wine. Southwind blends Southern hospitality and French winemaking. The winery's name reflects the Allens' Arkansas roots, and the selection of wines is driven by Lorre's love of French culture. Viticulturalist Jamie Sherman oversees grape cultivation.

The winery is in a heavily wooded area on a remote country road. The farm consists of a stately gray brick house with vineyards in the front, and a small but charming tasting room. Southwind specializes in the use of Lippizan horses, and offers horse boarding and hunter pacing. They are planning to build an underground cave that will be used for winemaking and tastings. My recommendation is to try Blood, Sweat & Tears, a Bordeaux-style wine made from Cabernet Sauvignon, Cabernet Franc, Merlot, and Chambourcin.

Address: 385 Lebanon Road (Route 654), Millville, NJ

Phone: (856) 391-5524

Website: southwindvineyardllc.com

E-mail: lorre@southwindvineyardllc.com

Appellation: Outer Coastal Plain

First vines planted: 2006

Opened to the public: 2012

Key people: Joseph Riley & Lorre Allen (owners); Jamie Sherman (viticulturalist)

Acres cultivated: 4

Cases/year: 800

Grapes: Cabernet Franc, Cabernet Sauvignon, Chambourcin, Chardonnay, Concord, Malbec, Merlot, Muscat Blanc, and Viognier

Other fruit: limes and peaches

Other attractions: horse boarding and riding, pet-friendly, picnicking

Days: tastings Tuesday to Sunday

Wineries Without Tasting Rooms

Vacchiano Farm and Swansea Vineyards do not have tasting rooms, and so I did not include them in road trips. Both have winery licenses from the state and produce very small quantities of wine that are sold by the bottle. I've never been able to obtain a bottle of Vacchiano's wine, and it's been some years since I tasted Swansea's wine, so my description of them is brief.

Vacchiano Farm:

Vacchiano Farm is located in the town of Washington in Warren County, and sells their meats, vegetables, cheese, pies, and sauces at outdoor markets in northern New Jersey. The farm grows over 25 different types of tomatoes, and all of their meat is free range. In 2004, Anthony Vacchiano Sr. and his son Anthony Vacciano Jr. planted grapes, and since 2009, they have sold a red table wine and a white table wine at the Montclair Farmers' Market.

Address: 135 Port Colden Road, Washington, NJ
Phone: 908-689-2227
Website: www.vacchianofarm.com
E-mail: N/A
Appellation: Warren Hills
First vines planted: 2004
Opened to the public: 2009
Key people: Anthony Vacchiano Sr., Anthony Vacciano Jr. (owners)
Acres cultivated: 11
Cases/year: minimal
Grapes: Chambourcin, Frontenac
Other fruit: N/A
Other products: breads, cheeses, fruits, meats, pies, sauces, vegetables

Swansea Vineyards:

Frank Baitinger planted grapes in Shiloh in 1994, and thirteen years later, Swansea Vineyards opened to the public. Named for the original settlers of Shiloh who were from Swansea, Wales, the winery had a tasting room and attended wine festivals for a few years, but now only sells their wine through a couple of nearby liquor stores. It is the only winery in New Jersey that produces wine from Lakemont and Reliance, which are seedless table grapes.

Address: 860 Main Street (Route 49), Shiloh, NJ
Phone: (856) 453-5778
Website: www.swanseavineyards.com
E-mail: jspiker@swanseavineyards.com
Appellation: Outer Coastal Plain
First vines planted: 1994
Opened to the public: 2007
Key people: Frank Baitinger (owner), Jennifer Spiker (general manager)
Acres cultivated: 12
Cases/year: minimal
Grapes: Cabernet Franc, Cabernet Sauvignon, Cayuga White, Chambourcin, Chardonnay, Lakemont, Merlot, Reliance, Traminette, and Vidal Blanc
Other fruit: apples, blackberries, blueberries, kiwifruit, nectarines, peaches, and strawberries

Appendix I – Appellations

An appellation is a legally-defined wine region (e.g., Bordeaux, Napa Valley). In the United States, appellations are referred to as American Viticultural Areas (AVAs), and have geographic boundaries drawn by the Alcohol and Tobacco Tax and Trade Bureau, an agency within the United States Department of the Treasury. For a winery to use a label advertising a particular appellation, 85% of the grapes most come from that region.

Appellations are supposed to encompass an area with similar climate, soil, and elevation, since those factors affect the taste of the wine. In practice, the delineation of AVAs is a highly controversial and often disputed process. The inclusion or exclusion of a winery from an AVA is in no way an indicator of a winery's quality. There are three AVAs currently defined for New Jersey, and a new AVA has been proposed for Cape May County.

Warren Hills:

This AVA covers 145,000 acres in Warren County. The Warren Hills region includes most of the county excluding a small area bordering Sussex County. The area consists of small valleys formed by tributaries of the Delaware River, and because of the way the water drains, most of the vineyards in the area are planted on southeast-facing slopes. Established in 1988, the AVA currently includes five wineries, and is primarily planted with French hybrid grapes.

Alba Vineyard	Vacchiano Farm
Brook Hollow Winery	Villa Milagro Vineyards
Four Sisters Winery	

Central Delaware Valley:

This appellation includes 96,000 acres in Pennsylvania and New Jersey, surrounding the Delaware River. Created in 1984, this AVAs covers parts of Hunterdon and Mercer counties. Several wineries that are no longer in business were in this appellation, but no current New Jersey winery is in the Central Delaware Valley AVA.

Outer Coastal Plain:

This huge AVA covers 2,250,000 acres in South Jersey, including all of Atlantic, Cape May, Cumberland, and Ocean counties and parts of Burlington, Camden, Gloucester, Monmouth, and Salem counties. The region is characterized by sandy soils and a mild climate influenced by the Atlantic Ocean and Delaware Bay. Though this region has 28 wineries, including the three oldest wineries in the state, this AVAs was not created until 2007. Many wineries located in this appellation are members of the Outer Coastal Plain Vineyard Association.

Amalthea Cellars	Monroeville Vineyard & Winery
Auburn Road Vineyards	Natali Vineyards
Balic Winery	Plagido's Winery
Bellview Winery	Renault Winery
Cape May Winery & Vineyard	Sharrott Winery
Chestnut Run Farm	Southwind Vineyard & Winery
Coda Rossa Winery	Summit City Farms & Winery
DeMastro Vineyards & Winery	Swansea Vineyards
DiBella Winery	Sylvin Farms Winery
DiMatteo Vineyards	Tomasello Winery
Hawk Haven Vineyard & Winery	Turdo Vineyards & Winery
Heritage Vineyards	Valenzano Winery
Jessie Creek Winery	Wagonhouse Winery
Laurita Winery	Willow Creek Winery

No appellation:

There are fifteen Garden State wineries that are not in an AVA. Central Jersey does not have a viticultural area, the majority of the wineries in the Skylands fall outside the boundaries of the Warren Hills and Central Delaware Valley regions, and two wineries near the Delaware River in the Farm Belt are not in the Outer Coastal Plain.

These wineries can label their products as "New Jersey wine," but cannot list a specific AVA. Keep in mind that the process of defining appellations can be arbitrary. For example, the five Warren County wineries are in an AVA, but the three wineries of Sussex County are not, despite both counties sharing similar weather and terrain.

Beneduce Vineyards
Cava Winery & Vineyard
Cedarvale Winery
Cream Ridge Winery
Four JG's Orchards & Vineyards
Hopewell Valley Vineyards
Mount Salem Vineyards
Old York Cellars

Peppadew Fresh Vineyards
Salem Oak Winery
Terhune Orchards
Unionville Vineyards
Ventimiglia Vineyard
Westfall Winery
Working Dog Winery

Cape May Peninsula (proposed):

This is a proposed appellation that would exclusively cover Cape May County. If created, the appellation would likely include the 397,000 acres of Cape May County. The proponents of this AVA note that Cape May County has far more frost-free days than other parts of the Outer Coastal Plain. If established, the six wineries of Cape May County will be within its borders.

Cape May Winery & Vineyard
Hawk Haven Vineyard & Winery
Jessie Creek Winery

Natali Vineyards
Turdo Vineyards & Winery
Willow Creek Winery

Appendix II – Winegrower Associations

Garden State Wine Growers Association (GSWGA):

Founded in 1980 as the Hunterdon Wine Growers Association, this group was instrumental in getting the New Jersey Farm Winery Act passed. Today, it's a state-wide organization of 41 wineries that provides its members with educational and marketing resources, advocates on wine-related legislative and regulatory issues, and sponsors festivals throughout the year.

Amalthea Cellars	Natali Vineyards
Auburn Road Vineyards	Old York Cellars
Bellview Winery	Peppadew Fresh Vineyards
Beneduce Vineyards	Plagido's Winery
Brook Hollow Winery	Renault Winery
Cape May Winery & Vineyard	Salem Oak Winery
Cava Winery and Vineyard	Sharrott Winery
Cedarvale Winery	Southwind Vineyard & Winery
Chestnut Run Farm	Summit City Farms & Winery
Coda Rossa Winery	Sylvin Farms Winery
Cream Ridge Winery	Terhune Orchards
DiBella Winery	Tomasello Winery
DiMatteo Vineyards	Unionville Vineyards
Four JG's Orchards & Vineyards	Valenzano Winery
Four Sisters Winery	Ventimiglia Vineyard
Hawk Haven Vineyard & Winery	Villa Milagro Vineyards
Heritage Vineyards	Wagonhouse Winery
Hopewell Valley Vineyards	Westfall Winery
Jessie Creek Winery	Willow Creek Winery
Laurita Winery	Working Dog Winery
Monroeville Vineyard & Winery	

Vintage North Jersey:

A subsidiary of the Garden State Wine Growers Association, Vintage North Jersey is a collaboration of 10 North Jersey wineries in Mercer, Hunterdon, Sussex, and Warren counties. Founded in 2013, the organization received a $16,000 tourism grant from the state to promote North Jersey vineyards and other local attractions near the wineries.

Beneduce Vineyards	Terhune Orchards
Brook Hollow Winery	Unionville Vineyards
Cava Winery and Vineyard	Ventimiglia Vineyard
Four Sisters Winery	Villa Milagro Vineyards
Old York Cellars	Westfall Winery

Outer Coastal Plain Vineyard Association (OCPVA):

This organization was founded in 2009 to promote the viability of grape growing in the Outer Coastal Plain. OCVPA includes 23 wineries, and a number of non-wine-producing vineyards.

Amalthea Cellars	Natali Vineyards
Auburn Road Vineyards	Plagido's Winery
Bellview Winery	Renault Winery
Cape May Winery & Vineyard	Sharrott Winery
Chestnut Run Farm	Southwind Vineyard & Winery
Coda Rossa Winery	Sylvin Farms Winery
Four JG's Orchards & Vineyards	Tomasello Winery
Hawk Haven Vineyard & Winery	Turdo Vineyards & Winery
Heritage Vineyards	Valenzano Winery
Jessie Creek Winery	Wagonhouse Winery
Laurita Winery	Willow Creek Winery
Monroeville Vineyard & Winery	

New Jersey Wine Industry Advisory Council:

This is an eight-person commission in the New Jersey Department of Agriculture that was founded in 1985 in order to assess and promote the state's wine industry. The group meets quarterly, and includes the Secretary of Agriculture, the Commissioner of Commerce and Economic Development, the Dean of Cook College at Rutgers University, four winery owners, and a viticulturalist.

Appendix III – Grape & Fruit Varieties

Wine is produced in New Jersey from 95 different grapes, and 29 other fruits. This list is still growing.

Albariño	Mourvèdre
Baco Noir	Muscat Blanc
Barbera	Muscat Of Alexandria
Blaufränkisch (Lemberger)	Muscat Ottonel
Brachetto	Nebbiolo
Cabernet Franc	Nero D'Avola
Cabernet Sauvignon	Niagara
Carignan	Noah
Catawba	Noiret
Cayuga White	Norton (Cynthiana)
Chambourcin	Orange Muscat
Chancellor	Petit Manseng
Chardonnay	Petit Verdot
Chenin Blanc	Pinotage
Ciliegiolo	Pinot Blanc
Colobel	Pinot Gris
Colombard	Pinot Noir
Concord	Rayon D'Or
Corot Noir	Reliance
Corvina	Riesling
Counoise	Rkatsiteli
De Chaunac	Rougeon
Delaware	Roussanne
Diamond	Sagrantino
Dolcetto	Sangiovese
Durif (Petite Sirah)	Sauvignon Blanc
Fredonia	Teroldego
Frontenac	Schiava Grossa
Frontenac Gris	Sémillon
Gewürztraminer	Seyval Blanc

Geneva Red
Grechetto
Grenache
Grüner Veltliner
Horizon
Ives Noir
La Crescent
Lagrein
Lakemont
Landot Noir
Léon Millot
Malbec
Malvasia Bianca
Marechal Foch
Marquette
Marquis
Marsanne
Merlot

St. Laurent
Sumoll
Syrah
Tempranillo
Tinta Cão
Touriga Nacional
Traminette
Trebbiano
Vespolina
Vidal Blanc
Vignoles (Ravat 51)
Villard Blanc
Villard Noir
Viognier
Vranec
Zinfandel
Zweigelt

açaí berries
almonds
apples
apricots
Asian pears
bananas
beach plums
black currants
blackberries
blueberries
cherries
cranberries
dandelions
honey (mead)
huckleberries

kiwifruit
limes
mangoes
nectarines
peaches
pears
pineapples
plums
pomegranates
pumpkins
raspberries
strawberries
sugar plums
watermelons

134

Appendix IV – Wine Festival & Events

Throughout the year, New Jersey wineries sponsor festivals and events. This chart includes every public event involving multiple wineries. Exact dates vary by year and not all wineries take part in every event so check in advance. Most of the festivals take place in an outdoor venue over a two-day weekend.

Wine trail weekends also take place on Saturday and Sunday, and involve visiting multiple wineries, each of whom puts their own spin on the wine trail theme. Beyond what is listed on this page, there are a countless number of events run by individual wineries.

Event	Location
Wine & Chocolate Weekend	Participating wineries
Spring Fever Wine & Food Tasting	Branches in West Long Branch
Mother's Day Wine Trail Weekend	Participating wineries
Pour Into Summer Wine Festival	Taylor Avenue in Beach Haven
Blues & Wine Festival	Natirar Park in Peapack-Gladstone
Medford Art, Wine & Music Festival	Main Street in Medford
Jersey Shore Wine Festival	First Energy Park in Lakewood
Wine & Music Festival	Sharrott Winery in Blue Anchor
Washington Lake Park Wine Festival	Washington Lake Park in Sewell
Win & Wine Weekend	Monmouth Park in Oceanport
Tropicana's Jersey Shore Festival	Tropicana Casino in Atlantic City
Barrel Trail Weekend	Participating wineries
Rutgers Gardens Wine Festival	Rutgers Gardens in New Brunswick
Two Bridges Wine Trail	Participating wineries in Farm Belt
Summer Chill Wine Festival	Renault Winery in Egg Harbor City
Demarest Farms Wine Festival	Demarest Farms in Hillsdale
Jazz It Up Wine Festival	Allaire State Park in Wall
Jersey Fresh Wine Festival	Burlington Fairground in Columbus
Festival of the Sea	Downtown Point Pleasant Beach
Jersey Skyline Wine Festival	Overpeck Park in Ridgefield Park
WineFest	Valenzano Winery in Shamong
Waterfront Wine & Food Festival	Lake Lenape Park in Mays Landing

Grand Harvest Wine Festival	Fosterfields Farm in Morristown
Cape May Wine Festival	Ferry Terminal in North Cape May
Stafford Fall Harvest Wine Festival	Manahawkin Park in Manahawkin
Autumn Wine Festival at RiverWinds	RiverWinds in West Deptford
Jake's Branch Autumn Wine Festival	Jakes Branch Park in Beachwood
Grape Adventure	Great Adventure in Jackson
Holiday Wine Trail Weekend	Participating wineries

Appendix V – Amenities

A winery owner once told me that 50% of his job was growing grapes and making wine, and the other 50% was being a good host. Keeping this in mind, a number of the state's vineyards permit picnicking, allow patrons to bring well-behaved pets, and are venues for weddings and other private events. A handful of wineries serve food, offer lodging, or sell other products besides wine.

Pet-Friendly:

Bellview Winery
Cape May Winery
Cream Ridge Winery
Four Sisters Winery
Hawk Haven Vineyard & Winery
Hopewell Valley Vineyards
Heritage Vineyards
Natali Vineyards
Salem Oak Vineyards

Southwind Vineyard & Winery
Tomasello Winery
Turdo Vineyards & Winery
Unionville Vineyards
Valenzano Winery
Ventimiglia Vineyard
Westfall Winery
Working Dog Winery

Picnicking:

Alba Vineyard
Amalthea Cellars
Bellview Winery
Beneduce Vineyards
Cape May Winery & Vineyard
Cedarvale Winery
Four Sisters Winery
Hawk Haven Vineyard & Winery
Heritage Vineyards
Hopewell Valley Vineyards
Natali Vineyards
Old York Cellars

Peppadew Fresh Vineyards
Salem Oak Vineyards
Terhune Orchards
Tomasello Winery
Unionville Vineyards
Valenzano Winery
Ventimiglia Vineyard
Villa Milagro Vineyards
Wagonhouse Winery
Westfall Winery
Willow Creek Winery
Working Dog Winery

Weddings:

Alba Vineyard
Amalthea Cellars
Auburn Road Vineyards
Bellview Winery
Beneduce Vineyards
Brook Hollow Winery
Cava Winery & Vineyard
Four Sisters Winery
Hopewell Valley Vineyards
Jessie Creek Winery
Laurita Winery
Natali Vineyards

Old York Cellars
Peppadew Fresh Vineyards
Renault Winery
Salem Oak Vineyards
Tomasello Winery
Turdo Vineyards & Winery
Unionville Vineyards
Valenzano Winery
Villa Milagro Vineyards
Willow Creek Winery
Working Dog Winery

Dining:

Auburn Road Vineyards – bistro; serves dinner on Friday nights
Cava Winery & Vineyard – bistro
Four Sisters Winery – bakery during autumn
Hopewell Valley Vineyards – serves pizzas on Fri. and Sat. nights
Laurita Winery – bistro
Renault Winery – two restaurants

Lodging:

Jessie Creek Winery – bed and breakfast
Laurita Winery – bed and winery
Renault Winery – hotel

Other Attractions:

Coda Rossa Winery – instructional winemaking
Four Sisters Winery – corn mazes, fruit picking

Heritage Vineyards – fruit picking, petting zoo
Laurita Winery – horseback riding
Old York Cellars – art gallery
Renault Winery – golf course
Sharrott Winery – solar-powered
Southwind Vineyard & Winery – horse boarding and riding
Summit City Farms & Winery – pony rides
Terhune Orchards – fruit picking, wagon rides
Turdo Vineyards & Winery – solar-powered
Valenzano Winery – solar-powered
Villa Milagro Vineyards – organic wines, tourist train
Westfall Winery – horse boarding

Other Products:

Hopewell Valley Vineyards – olive oil

Peppadew Fresh Vineyards – azaleas, flowering quinces, hydrangeas, peppadews, pussywillows

Summit City Farms & Winery – fruits, vegetables

Terhune Orchards – bread, cider, doughnuts, flowers, fruits, herbs, pies, vegetables

Vacchiano Farm – breads, cheeses, fruits, meats, pies, sauces, vegetables

Willow Creek Winery – eggs, flowers, fruits, honey, poultry, tobacco, vegetables, wormwood

Appendix VI – Statistics

The following is a compilation of the 48 wineries of New Jersey, listing the year grapes were first planted for commercial use, the year when the wine was first sold to the public, the number of acres planted with grapes, and the number of cases of wine (2.38 gallons per case) produced each year.

Name	Planted	Opened	Acres	Cases
Alba Vineyard	1980	1982	42	11,000
Amalthea Cellars	1976	1981	10	5,000
Auburn Road Vineyards	2004	2007	19	4,200
Balic Winery	1800s	1966	57	N/A
Bellview Winery	2000	2001	40	8,000
Beneduce Vineyards	2009	2012	10	3,000
Brook Hollow Winery	2002	2007	8	1,050
Cape May Winery & Vineyard	1992	1995	25	11,000
Cava Winery & Vineyard	2005	2008	5	3,000
Cedarvale Winery	2004	2008	8	2,500
Chestnut Run Farm	1986	2007	5	700
Coda Rossa Winery	2002	2010	10	1,500
Cream Ridge Winery	1987	1988	14	5,000
DeMastro Vineyards & Winery	1991	2009	4	300
DiBella Winery	2002	2010	4	900
DiMatteo Vineyards	2000	2002	14	1,500
Four JG's Orchards & Vineyards	1999	2004	40	2,500
Four Sisters Winery	1981	1984	8	5,000
Hawk Haven Vineyard & Winery	1997	2009	9	4,200
Heritage Vineyards	1998	2002	40	13,000
Hopewell Valley Vineyards	2001	2003	25	6,000
Jessie Creek Winery	2002	2012	5	1,200
Laurita Winery	1998	2008	44	14,000

Monroeville Vineyard & Winery	2010	2012	4	1,800
Mount Salem Vineyards	2005	2010	7	1,000
Natali Vineyards	2001	2007	7	1,800
Old York Cellars	1978	2010	12	3,600
Peppadew Fresh Vineyards	2011	2012	4	900
Plagido's Winery	1999	2007	14	4,200
Renault Winery	1864	1870	48	20,000
Salem Oak Winery	2003	2013	4	900
Sharrott Winery	2005	2008	6	7,000
Southwind Vineyard & Winery	2007	2012	4	800
Summit City Farms & Winery	2013	2014	15	700
Swansea Vineyards	1994	2007	12	Minimal
Sylvin Farms Winery	1977	1985	11	1,000
Terhune Orchards	2003	2010	5	1,100
Tomasello Winery	1888	1933	70	65,000
Turdo Vineyards & Winery	1999	2004	5	1,100
Unionville Vineyards	1988	1993	54	8,500
Vacchiano Farm	2004	2009	11	Minimal
Valenzano Winery	1991	1996	44	40,000
Ventimiglia Vineyard	2002	2008	5	1,000
Villa Milagro Vineyards	2003	2007	11	1,500
Wagonhouse Winery	2004	2005	10	7,000
Westfall Winery	2000	2003	6	9,000
Willow Creek Winery	2005	2012	40	6,000
Working Dog Winery	2001	2003	16	3,500